Reflections of
God's New Testament Books

JULIE RYAN

WestBow
P R E S S®
A DIVISION OF THOMAS NELSON
& ZONDERVAN

This book is a work of non-fiction. Unless otherwise noted, the author
and the publisher make no explicit guarantees as to the accuracy of
the information contained in this book and in some cases, names of
people and places have been altered to protect their privacy.

WestBow Press books may be ordered through booksellers or by contacting:

WestBow Press
A Division of Thomas Nelson & Zondervan
1663 Liberty Drive
Bloomington, IN 47403
www.westbowpress.com
844-714-3454

Scripture quotations are taken from the Holy Bible, New Living Translation,
copyright © 1996, 2004, 2007 by Tyndale House Foundation. Used by permission
of Tyndale House Publishers, Inc., Carol Stream, Illinois 60188. All rights reserved.

ISBN: 979-8-3850-0727-1 (sc)
ISBN: 979-8-3850-0728-8 (e)

Library of Congress Control Number: 2023917756

Print information available on the last page.

WestBow Press rev. date: 09/15/2023

I will study your commandments
and reflect on your ways.
Psalm 119:15

Heavenly Father,
As I reflect on your Word,
help me to understand and apply
your truths to my life.
In Jesus' name I pray,

Amen

CONTENTS

Matthew

Matthew 1 1

Matthew 2 2

Matthew 3 3

Matthew 4 4

Matthew 5 5

Matthew 6 6

Matthew 7 7

Matthew 8 9

Matthew 9 10

Matthew 10 11

Matthew 11 12

Matthew 12 13

Matthew 13 14

Matthew 14 15

Matthew 15 16

Matthew 16 17

Matthew 17 18

Matthew 18 19

Matthew 19 20

Matthew 20 21

Matthew 21 22

Matthew 22 23

Matthew 23 24

Matthew 24... 25
Matthew 25... 26
Matthew 26... 27
Matthew 27... 28
Matthew 28... 30

Mark

Mark 1 33
Mark 2 34
Mark 3 35
Mark 4 36
Mark 5 37
Mark 6 38
Mark 7 39
Mark 8 40
Mark 9 41
Mark 10 42
Mark 11 43
Mark 12 44
Mark 13 45
Mark 14 46
Mark 15 47
Mark 16 48

Luke

Luke 1 51
Luke 2 52
Luke 3 53

Luke 4 54
Luke 5 55
Luke 6 56
Luke 7 57
Luke 8 58
Luke 9 59
Luke 10 60
Luke 11 61
Luke 12 62
Luke 13 63
Luke 14 64
Luke 15 65
Luke 16 66
Luke 17 67
Luke 18 68
Luke 19 69
Luke 20 70
Luke 21 71
Luke 22 72
Luke 23 73
Luke 24 74

John

John 1 77
John 2 78
John 3 79
John 4 80
John 5 81

John 6 82
John 7 83
John 8 84
John 9 85
John 10 86
John 11 87
John 12 88
John 13 89
John 14 90
John 15 91
John 16 92
John 17 93
John 18 94
John 19 95
John 20 96
John 21 97

Acts

Acts 1 101
Acts 2 102
Acts 3 103
Acts 4 104
Acts 5 105
Acts 6 106
Acts 7 107
Acts 8 108
Acts 9 109
Acts 10 110

Acts 11 111
Acts 12 112
Acts 13 113
Acts 14 114
Acts 15 115
Acts 16 116
Acts 17 117
Acts 18 118
Acts 19 119
Acts 20 120
Acts 21 121
Acts 22 122
Acts 23 123
Acts 24 124
Acts 25 125
Acts 26 126
Acts 27 127
Acts 28 128

Romans

Romans 1 131
Romans 2 132
Romans 3 133
Romans 4 134
Romans 5 135
Romans 6 136
Romans 7 137
Romans 8 138

Romans 9 139
Romans 10 140
Romans 11 141
Romans 12 142
Romans 13 143
Romans 14 144
Romans 15 145
Romans 16 146

1 Corinthians

1 Corinthians 1 149
1 Corinthians 2 150
1 Corinthians 3 151
1 Corinthians 4 152
1 Corinthians 5 153
1 Corinthians 6 154
1 Corinthians 7 155
1 Corinthians 8 156
1 Corinthians 9 157
1 Corinthians 10 158
1 Corinthians 11 159
1 Corinthians 12 160
1 Corinthians 13 161
1 Corinthians 14 163
1 Corinthians 15 164
1 Corinthians 16 165

2 Corinthians

2 Corinthians 1 169
2 Corinthians 2 170
2 Corinthians 3 171
2 Corinthians 4 172
2 Corinthians 5 173
2 Corinthians 6 174
2 Corinthians 7 175
2 Corinthians 8 176
2 Corinthians 9 177
2 Corinthians 10 178
2 Corinthians 11 179
2 Corinthians 12 180
2 Corinthians 13 181

Galatians

Galatians 1 185
Galatians 2 186
Galatians 3 187
Galatians 4 188
Galatians 5 189
Galatians 6 190

Ephesians

Ephesians 1 193
Ephesians 2 195
Ephesians 3 196

Ephesians 4 197
Ephesians 5 198
Ephesians 6 199

Philippians

Philippians 1 203
Philippians 2 204
Philippians 3 205
Philippians 4 206

Colossians

Colossians 1 209
Colossians 2 210
Colossians 3 211
Colossians 4 212

1 Thessalonians

1 Thessalonians 1 215
1 Thessalonians 2 216
1 Thessalonians 3 217
1 Thessalonians 4 218
1 Thessalonians 5 219

2 Thessalonians

2 Thessalonians 1 223
2 Thessalonians 2 224
2 Thessalonians 3 225

1 Timothy

1 Timothy 1 229
1 Timothy 2 230
1 Timothy 3 231
1 Timothy 4 232
1 Timothy 5 233
1 Timothy 6 234

2 Timothy

2 Timothy 1 237
2 Timothy 2 238
2 Timothy 3 239
2 Timothy 4 240

Titus

Titus 1 243
Titus 2 244
Titus 3 245

Philemon

Philemon 249

Hebrews

Hebrews 1 253
Hebrews 2 254
Hebrews 3 255
Hebrews 4 256

Hebrews 5 257
Hebrews 6 258
Hebrews 7 259
Hebrews 8 260
Hebrews 9 261
Hebrews 10 262
Hebrews 11 263
Hebrews 12 264
Hebrews 13 265

James

James 1 269
James 2 270
James 3 271
James 4 272
James 5 273

1 Peter

1 Peter 1 277
1 Peter 2 278
1 Peter 3 279
1 Peter 4 280
1 Peter 5 281

2 Peter

2 Peter 1 285
2 Peter 2 286
2 Peter 3 287

1 John

1 John 1 291
1 John 2 292
1 John 3 293
1 John 4 294
1 John 5 295

2 John

2 John 299

3 John

3 John 303

Jude

Jude 307

Revelation

Revelation 1 311
Revelation 2 313
Revelation 3 315
Revelation 4 316
Revelation 5 318
Revelation 6 319
Revelation 7 321
Revelation 8 322
Revelation 9 324
Revelation 10 325

Revelation 11 326
Revelation 12 328
Revelation 13 330
Revelation 14 332
Revelation 15 334
Revelation 16 335
Revelation 17 337
Revelation 18 338
Revelation 19 339
Revelation 20 340
Revelation 21 342
Revelation 22 344

✧ ✧ ✧

The Book of
MATTHEW

MATTHEW 1

Passage: "This is a record of the ancestors of Jesus the Messiah, a descendant of David and of Abraham."

Reflection:

The ancestors of Jesus were not perfect people. They varied from a prostitute to kings. They included Israelites and a Moabite. They were poor and rich. They lived in tents and palaces. The ancestors of the Messiah probably looked a lot like the people in your family tree.

In fulfillment of the prophetic message of Isaiah, Immanuel (God is with us) was born of a virgin.

He was fully man.

The Messiah was conceived through the power of the Holy Spirit.

He was fully God.

Jesus (the Lord saves) was born to die—to save people from their sins.

He was God in a human body.

MATTHEW 2

Passage: "This fulfilled what the Lord had spoken through the prophet."

Reflection:

Micah prophesied that the Messiah would be born in Bethlehem. Jesus was born in Bethlehem.

Jeremiah prophesied that the children in and around Bethlehem would be killed. King Herod killed all the boys who were two years old and under in an attempt to kill Jesus.

Hosea prophesied that God would call his Son out of Egypt. Jesus lived in Egypt with Mary and Joseph until Herod died, and then God called them to move back to Israel.

Joseph, Mary, and Jesus returned to their hometown of Nazareth, making Jesus, the Messiah, a Nazarene — just as the prophets said.

Because God is the author of everything from the beginning to the end of time, he knows exactly how each day will unfold before it even starts. So when God spoke through the Old Testament prophets about the things that would take place concerning his Son, Jesus the Messiah, it only stands to reason that they would happen just as he said.

MATTHEW 3

Passage: In those days, John the Baptist came to the Judean wilderness and began preaching. His message was, "Repent of your sins and turn to God, for the Kingdom of Heaven is near."

Reflection:

Not until a person repents of their sins and turns to God is baptism with water to be done. Not until a person repents of their sins and turns to God are they baptized with the Holy Spirit. And not until a person repents of their sins and turns to Jesus, God's dearly loved Son, do they become true children of God.

Baptism is not salvation. It is something that is done in obedience to God. Baptism is outward expression that we are saved, not because of who our ancestors are, but because we have confessed our sins and turned to God through Jesus.

MATTHEW 4

Passage: "And for those who lived in the land where death casts its shadow, a light has shined."

Reflection:

Jesus' ministry started after John the Baptist was arrested. The Messiah fulfilled another prophecy from Isaiah when he went to Zebulun and Naphtali in Galilee to shine his great light to the people living in spiritual darkness.

God prepared Jesus for his ministry during forty days of solitude and fasting. Jesus went where the Father told him to go. He preached what the Father told him to preach. He trained the people that the Father had chosen to be his disciples. And he healed all whom the Father told him to heal. Because Jesus was obedient to the will of God the Father, his ministry was successful in every way.

MATTHEW 5

Passage: "God blesses those who are poor and realize their need for him, for the Kingdom of Heaven is theirs."

Reflection:

Without recognizing your spiritual poverty and your need for a Savior, you will not inherit the Kingdom of Heaven.

Without accepting Jesus Christ into your heart, you will not be the salt of the earth or the light of the world. You will continue to live in darkness.

Without following Jesus, despite those who mock and persecute you for doing so, you will not receive a great reward in heaven.

Without being a true child of the Father in heaven, you are not able to control your anger, love your enemies, or pray for those who persecute you.

When you realize your need for Jesus and humbly receive him as your Savior and Lord, you will see God's supernatural power at work in you. He will enable you to live the Christian life on earth while you look forward to your future home—the Kingdom of Heaven.

MATTHEW 6

Passage: "Seek the Kingdom of God above all else, and live righteously, and he will give you everything you need."

Reflection:

Don't seek to be recognized and admired by people but seek your reward from God who sees and hears everything you do.

Don't refuse to forgive others, but forgive those who sin against you, and God will forgive you for your sins.

Don't store up treasures on earth but store your treasures in heaven. Your heart will be where your treasures are stored—with God or money.

Don't worry about everyday life. Live one day at a time, have faith in God, and put him first—and he will give you everything you need and more!

MATTHEW 7

Passage: "Do to others whatever you would like them to do to you. This is the essence of all that is taught in the law and the prophets."

Reflection:

Do not judge others, and you will not be judged. Deal with your own issues before trying to fix the problems that you think others have.

Children of God can ask their heavenly Father for anything. He loves to give us good gifts. So don't stop asking, seeking, knocking, praying.

Only a few people will ever find Jesus—the only gateway to the Kingdom of God and eternal life. But many will choose the highway to hell. So don't try to force Jesus on people who don't want to listen—don't waste what is holy on people who are not holy—it's like throwing pearls to pigs.

People who act religious on the outside but have never received Jesus on the inside—false disciples—will be told by Jesus on judgment day, "I never knew you. Get away from me." They will be chopped down and thrown into the fire.

But anyone who hears and obeys Jesus, anyone who builds their life on the solid Rock, and anyone who produces good fruit will still be standing after the storms of life have passed. They will be welcomed into the Kingdom of Heaven.

MATTHEW 8

Passage: This fulfilled the word of the Lord through the prophet Isaiah, who said, "He took our sicknesses and removed our diseases."

Reflection:

Jesus demonstrated his power over physical illness—healing a man with leprosy, a woman with a fever, and a man who was paralyzed. He demonstrated his power over spiritual illness—casting out evil spirits from demon-possessed men. Jesus even demonstrated his power over nature—rebuking the wind and waves and instantly calming the storm on the lake.

Jesus has the power to heal you, too—from the sickness and death caused by sin. If you admit that you are a sinner and believe in Jesus, he will cleanse you of all your sins. You will no longer be spiritually dead, but you will be filled with the eternal life of the Holy Spirit of God. So you will no longer need to fear being thrown into the outer darkness of hell where there is weeping and gnashing of teeth, but instead, you can look forward to inheriting the Kingdom of Heaven.

Passage: Jesus turned around, and when he saw her, he said, "Daughter, be encouraged! Your faith has made you well."

Reflection:

Some people think they are made righteous because of what they do—by going to church, following laws, performing rituals, and offering sacrifices. Jesus didn't come to patch up the old way of doing things; he came to bring an entirely new way of becoming righteous—through faith in him.

Seeing their faith, Jesus healed the paralyzed man.

Because of her faith, Jesus made the woman with the blood condition well.

Because of the faith of the synagogue leader, Jesus brought his daughter back to life.

Because they believed, Jesus opened the eyes of the two blind men.

And because of faith in Jesus, a man who was demon-possessed and couldn't speak was freed of the demon and began to speak.

Jesus has compassion for people who are confused and helpless, like sheep without a shepherd. He came to show mercy and heal sinners in response to their faith in him.

MATTHEW 10

Passage: "Don't be afraid of those who want to kill your body; they cannot touch your soul. Fear only God, who can destroy both soul and body in hell."

Reflection:

Like the twelve disciples, we are to spread the Good News about the Kingdom of Heaven. But there is a cost to being a follower of Jesus.

Since Jesus has been called the prince of demons, those who belong to him will be called by even worse names. You may be arrested and handed over to the courts to stand trial. You may be flogged with whips in synagogues. You may be betrayed. You may be persecuted and have to flee. And all nations will hate you because you are a follower of Jesus. But don't be afraid and don't cling to your life, or you will lose it. Give up your life for Jesus, and you will find it.

Go tell unbelievers about Jesus.

Shout it for all to hear,

"Repent of your sins and turn to God,
for the Kingdom of Heaven is near!"

MATTHEW 11

Passage: John the Baptist, who was in prison, heard about all the things the Messiah was doing. So he sent his disciples to ask Jesus, "Are you the Messiah we've been expecting, or should we keep looking for someone else?"

Reflection:

Is Jesus the Messiah?

The blind see, the lame walk, the lepers are cured, the deaf hear, and the dead are raised to life. The Good News is being preached, and the Kingdom of Heaven has been forcefully advancing even though violent people continue to attack it.

Jesus is the Messiah.

He is the Son of God who reveals the Father to those with childlike faith. Unbelievers, who refuse to repent and accept him as their Savior and Lord, will go down to the place of the dead. So come to him. He will give you rest. Take his yoke—it is easy to bear, and your burden will be light. Let him teach you, for he is humble and gentle at heart.

Yes, Jesus is the Messiah!

MATTHEW 12

Passage: "For as Jonah was in the belly of the great fish for three days and three nights, so will the Son of Man be in the heart of the earth for three days and three nights."

Reflection:

Jesus, the Son of Man, is Lord—even over the Sabbath. He is our rest.

Jesus knows what people are thinking and planning. He is omniscient.

Jesus is God's chosen servant, as prophesied by Isaiah. He is the Messiah.

Jesus is stronger than Satan, whose kingdom will be destroyed. He is returning.

Jesus predicted his resurrection after being in the heart of the earth for three days and three nights. He is alive and well.

Jesus is the brother of anyone who does the will of his Father and repents of their sins. Is Jesus your brother?

MATTHEW 13

Passage: "Jesus always used stories and illustrations when speaking to the crowds. In fact, he never spoke to them without using such parables. This fulfilled what God had spoken through the prophet."

Reflection:

One parable that Jesus told was about the wheat and the weeds.

Jesus pictures himself as the farmer. His field is the world. The good seed of wheat represents the people who belong to God. And the weeds are the people who have rejected Jesus, so they belong to the devil who continues to plant weeds among the wheat. The harvest is the end of the world, and the harvesters are the angels.

"Just as the weeds are sorted out and burned in the fire, so it will be at the end of the world. The Son of Man will send his angels, and they will remove from his Kingdom everything that causes sin and all who do evil. And the angels will throw them into the fiery furnace, where there will be weeping and gnashing of teeth. Then the righteous will shine like the sun in their Father's Kingdom. Anyone with ears to hear should listen and understand!"

Any questions?

Reading:

MATTHEW 14

Passage: "But we have only five loaves and two fish!" they answered.

Reflection:

When the disciples gave Jesus the five loaves of bread and two fish they had, the Lord turned it into a meal for 5,000 men plus women and children!

When we have a problem and we look only to ourselves and our resources, it may seem impossible. But when we give what little we have to Jesus in faith, he can turn it into something much more than we imagined.

When Peter saw Jesus walking on the water, he asked Jesus to let him do it, too. Jesus said, "Yes, come." Peter had enough faith to get out of his boat and walk on the water toward Jesus! But when he took his eyes off Jesus and focused on the storm, he started to sink. Jesus immediately saved Peter when he called.

Do you have enough faith to get out of your boat and walk to Jesus? If so, keep your focus on him so you don't start to sink. But if you do lose your focus when problems arise like storms, call out to Jesus and he will save you—immediately.

MATTHEW 15

Passage: "These people honor me with their lips, but their hearts are far from me."

Reflection:

When man-made ideas violate the commands of God, we are the ones who have a problem. When people cancel the Word of God for the sake of traditions, their worship is a farce. And when your heart is defiled, so are the words you speak.

But when your faith is great, Jesus will grant your requests. When you bring him your problems, you will be amazed at what he does. And when you accept the broken bread of Jesus, symbolizing his broken body, your soul will be satisfied forever.

MATTHEW 16

Passage: "And what do you benefit if you gain the whole world but lose your own soul? Is anything worth more than your soul?"

Reflection:

The resurrection of Jesus from the grave—the sign of the prophet Jonah—has been given to us by God. There is no need for more miraculous signs to prove that Jesus is the Messiah. So beware of deceptive teaching about Jesus Christ, for it spreads like yeast in bread into the minds of the people who hear it.

Like Jesus revealed to his disciples that he would be killed and raised from the dead on the third day, God will reveal the truth about his Son to people with sincere hearts. Those who accept the truth will save their soul, but those who reject it will lose their soul.

So, who do you say Jesus is? Your answer will determine your eternity.

MATTHEW 17

Passage: But even as he spoke, a bright cloud overshadowed them, and a voice from the cloud said, "This is my dearly loved Son, who brings me great joy. Listen to him."

Reflection:

Jesus told the disciples that he would be betrayed into the hands of his enemies. Listen to him.

Jesus said that he would suffer and be killed. Listen to him.

And Jesus said that he would be raised from the dead. Listen to him.

Have faith in Jesus, even faith the size of a mustard seed, and you can move mountains. Nothing will be impossible—if you listen to him.

MATTHEW 18

Passage: Then he said, "I tell you the truth, unless you turn from your sins and become like little children, you will never get into the Kingdom of Heaven."

Reflection:

The world tempts people and causes them to fall into sin. But it is not God's will that anyone should perish and be thrown into the eternal fire of hell. So he sent Jesus to search for the spiritually lost, like sheep who have wandered away, and rescue them.

When we humble ourselves like a child and fall down before the King in repentance, we are forgiven of our sin debt—a debt so large that it could never be paid by our efforts. We are mercifully released to live in freedom from sin. And we will be welcomed into the Kingdom of Heaven as a child of God!

MATTHEW 19

Passage: Jesus looked at them intently and said, "Humanly speaking, it is impossible. But with God, everything is possible."

Reflection:

With God, even a rich person can enter the Kingdom of Heaven.

With God, those who seem the least important now will be the greatest when the world is made new.

With God, children are taken to heaven when they die.

With God, there is only One who is good.

With God, people are made male and female from the beginning.

With God, marriage is between a man and a woman.

With God, when you give money to the poor, you will have treasure in heaven.

With God, anyone can be saved.

With God, nothing is impossible.

MATTHEW 20

Passage: "For even the Son of Man came not to be served but to serve others and to give his life as a ransom for many."

Reflection:

Jesus came to serve others, like the blind men that he served when he healed them. When Jesus touched their eyes, they could see instantly! Not a day later, not gradually, but completely and instantly. So it is when a person receives God's gift of salvation—they are saved completely and instantly. And it doesn't matter how long you are a follower of Jesus before you enter the Kingdom of Heaven. Those who have been believers the longest will not necessarily get more than a new believer. Jesus is kind, and he will decide who receives what.

Jesus came to give his life as a ransom for many. Again, Jesus told his disciples that he was going to be crucified, but on the third day, he would be raised from the dead. Jesus came down from heaven and took on a human body so that he could offer himself to God as a perfect sacrifice for our sins. The Son of God came to pay the price for our sins and deliver us from punishment, setting free all who believe in him.

MATTHEW 21

Passage: "I tell you, the Kingdom of God will be taken away from you and given to a nation that will produce the proper fruit."

Reflection:

The leading priests and Pharisees were wicked in their hearts, like the wicked farmers in the parable that Jesus told. They refused to believe Jesus, they did not accept his authority, they refused to repent of their sins, and they did not acknowledge Jesus as their King. Even after seeing his miracles, they rejected Jesus and wanted to arrest him. They were like the fig tree with no fruit—cursed by God to wither and die. They, and people like them, will not get into the Kingdom of God.

MATTHEW 22

Passage: "For many are called, but few are chosen."

Reflection:

In the parable of the Great Feast, the people of Israel were the first to be invited by God to enter the Kingdom of Heaven, but most refused to believe that Jesus was the Messiah. They ignored God's servants who shared the truth with them. They went on their own way, doing their own thing, focusing on works and the priorities of this world. Even today, some messengers of God are increasingly insulted and even killed, like Jesus was, by those who hate God's Son.

So God is now inviting everyone—good and bad, Jew and Gentile—to the wedding feast that will be held in the Kingdom of Heaven. But the guests who are not dressed in clothes of righteousness, provided only to those who belong to Jesus, will be thrown into outer darkness, where there will be weeping and gnashing of teeth.

MATTHEW 23

Passage: "So practice and obey whatever they tell you, but don't follow their example. For they don't practice what they teach."

Reflection:

Many teachers of religion look like righteous people, but inwardly their hearts are filled with hypocrisy and lawlessness. Jesus described these people as hypocrites, blind guides, blind fools, whitewashed tombs, snakes, and sons of vipers! Everything they do is for show. They crush people with unbearable religious demands while they ignore the more important things like justice, mercy, and faith.

God in heaven is our only spiritual Father, and we who belong to Christ are brothers and sisters. So we should practice and obey what Jesus tells us and follow his perfect example, for the Messiah is our only teacher.

MATTHEW 24

Passage: "Now learn a lesson from the fig tree. When its branches bud and its leaves begin to sprout, you know that summer is near. In the same way, when you see all these things, you can know his return is very near, right at the door."

Reflection:

Many will come in Jesus' name claiming to be the Messiah. There will be wars and threats of wars. There will be famines and earthquakes in many parts of the world. Christians will be arrested, persecuted, and killed. Two people will be working together—one will be taken, and the other left. Sin will be rampant everywhere. The love of many will grow cold. And the Good News about the Kingdom will be preached throughout the whole world so that all nations will hear it. And then the end will come.

Like it was in Noah's day, most people didn't realize what was going to happen until the flood came and swept them all away. So we must be ready all the time, for Jesus will return when we least expect it.

MATTHEW 25

Passage: "To those who use well what they are given, even more will be given, and they will have an abundance. But from those who do nothing, even what little they have will be taken away."

Reflection:

When Jesus returns, everyone must stand before him and give an account of how they used their life. We will be judged according to what we did with what we were given—our knowledge, opportunities, talents, time, and treasure. Did we hear the gospel and accept Jesus as our Savior? Or did we do nothing? Did we lead a godly life? Or did we do nothing? Did we serve the Lord by serving others? Or did we do nothing?

Jesus will then separate the sheep—those who belong to him—from the goats. The sheep are blessed by the Father and will inherit the Kingdom. But the goats are cursed and will go away into the eternal fire prepared for the devil and his demons. The sheep are righteous and will go into eternal life. But the goats are wicked and will go away into eternal punishment. The sheep will hear Jesus say, "Well done, my good and faithful servant—let's celebrate together!"

Reading:

MATTHEW 26

Passage: "My Father! If it is possible, let this cup of suffering be taken away from me. Yet I want your will to be done, not mine."

Reflection:

Betrayed by Judas, deserted by his other disciples, denied by Peter, and falsely accused. Jesus knew what it was like to suffer. Yet he willingly subjected himself to this, even though he could have asked his Father to send thousands of angels to protect him.

Jesus came to give his body and his blood as a sacrifice to forgive the sins of many, and he knew that he would have to drink the cup of suffering to accomplish God's will. Those who accept Jesus as the Messiah, the Son of God, will be reunited with him. But those who reject Jesus as their Savior will go away, weeping bitterly.

MATTHEW 27

Passage: "I have sinned," Judas declared, "for I have betrayed an innocent man."

Reflection:

Judas betrayed him.

The leading priests picked up the coins. "It wouldn't be right to put this money in the Temple treasury," they said, "since it was payment for murder."

The leading priests paid for Jesus to be murdered.

"Which one do you want me to release to you— Barabbas, or Jesus, who is called the Messiah?"

Pilot knew very well that the religious leaders had arrested Jesus out of envy.

"Leave that innocent man alone. I suffered through a terrible nightmare about him last night."

Pilot's wife knew that Jesus was an innocent man.

"I am innocent of this man's blood. The responsibility is yours!"

Pilot washed his hands of the people's decision to crucify Jesus.

They knelt before him in mockery and taunted, "Hail! King of the Jews!" And they spit on him and grabbed the stick and struck him on the head.

The soldiers mocked Jesus.

"If you are the Son of God, save yourself and come down from the cross!"

The people shouted abuse, shaking their heads in mockery.

"He saved others," they scoffed, "but he can't save himself! So he is the King of Israel, is he?"

The leading priests, the teachers of religious law, and the elders also mocked Jesus. And the revolutionaries who were crucified with him ridiculed him in the same way.

What will you do with Jesus, who is called the Messiah?

MATTHEW 28

Passage: "Early on Sunday morning, as the new day was dawning..."

Reflection:

The angel of the Lord came down from heaven, rolled aside the stone at Jesus' tomb—not so Jesus could get out, but so people could get in—and sat on it.

The tomb guards shook with fear and fainted.

The angel told both Marys, "Don't be afraid! I know you are looking for Jesus, who was crucified. He isn't here! He is risen from the dead, just as he said would happen. Come, see where his body was lying."

The women ran, filled with great joy, to tell the disciples the angel's message.

The leading priests bribed the guards to say that Jesus' body was stolen during the night by his disciples.

The disciples met Jesus in Galilee and worshiped him.

And Jesus said, "I have been given all authority in Heaven and on earth. Therefore, go and make disciples of all the nations, baptizing them in the name of the Father and the Son and the Holy Spirit. Teach these new disciples to obey all the commands I have given you. And be sure of this: I am with you always, even to the end of the age."

Resurrection Sunday! What an action-packed, emotional, glorious, and victorious day! Hallelujah! Jesus is alive!

✧ ✧ ✧

The Book of
MARK

MARK 1

Passage: "The Spirit then compelled Jesus to go into the wilderness, where he was tempted by Satan for forty days. He was out among the wild animals, and angels took care of him."

Reflection:

God allowed Jesus to be tested by Satan through temptation for forty days. So it shouldn't be surprising that we, as children of God, must also endure testing in the form of trials, tribulation, and temptation.

Sometimes, God will take us into our own wilderness situations. But God's goal is to see how we will respond to these circumstances, to take us deeper and further than we could go on our own, and to make us victorious in Jesus. Satan's goal is to defeat us.

Evil spirits and demons still exist, and they know who Jesus is and who belongs to him. Although evil spirits cannot possess us, they can harass us. Destroying Christians, preventing us from telling others about Jesus, and ruining our testimony is still the plan and purpose of Satan's spiritual warfare.

It may feel like we are out among the wild animals, but we have Jesus and angels to take care of us. So don't be discouraged, for the battle is not yours, but God's!

MARK 2

Passage: "There were many people of this kind among
            Jesus' followers."

Reflection:
    Followers of Jesus know they are sinners.
    Followers of Jesus were called scum by those who
think they are righteous.
    Followers of Jesus had bad reputations.
    Followers of Jesus were spiritually sick.
    Followers of Jesus were paralyzed by sin.
    Followers of Jesus bring others to him.
    Followers of Jesus have faith in the Lord.
    Followers of Jesus recognize their need for a Savior.
    Followers of Jesus have been forgiven and healed.
    Followers of Jesus listen to him.
    Followers of Jesus put the needs of people first.
    Followers of Jesus are just like you and me.

MARK 3

Passage: "He looked around at them angrily and was deeply saddened by their hard hearts."

Reflection:

Jesus' enemies, the teachers of religious law, were perfect examples of people with hard hearts. They allowed rules, like not working on the Sabbath, to prevent them from doing good deeds, like healing a person on the Sabbath. They put laws before love. They destroyed life instead of saving it. They put evil before good.

The hearts of the teachers of religious law were so hard that they blocked all flow of faith needed to believe in Jesus and to come close to God. They even blasphemed the Holy Spirit by calling him an evil spirit. These people, and people like them, will never be forgiven and will suffer eternal consequences.

MARK 4

Passage: Then he asked them, "Why are you afraid? Do you still have no faith?"

Reflection:

God allowed a fierce storm to occur when the disciples were trying to cross to the other side of the lake. The waves were breaking into the boat, and it began to fill with water. The disciples were absolutely terrified! But they forgot one important detail—Jesus was in the boat with them.

So when God allows problems to come storming into our lives and spill over into our place of comfort and safety, we must remember that Jesus is here with us. We can call out to him with prayers of faith, and he will rebuke the wind and calm the waves. Let your heart be still. Fear and faith cannot exist in the same boat.

MARK 5

Passage: "Please come and lay your hands on her; heal her so she can live."

Reflection:

Jesus heals in response to faith. He healed a demon-possessed man, a bleeding woman, and a little girl who had died! Although we cannot physically touch Jesus like these people did, he is still able to heal us.

Jesus said, "Don't be afraid. Just have faith." If you have put your faith in Jesus as your Savior, God has already healed you spiritually. He resurrected your dead spirit to eternal life, and his Holy Spirit dwells inside you. Maybe it is God's plan to heal you in other ways, too. If he has given you the faith to pray for this, then keep on asking. And if he does heal you, go in peace and proclaim the great things Jesus has done for you!

MARK 6

Passage: But Jesus spoke to them at once. "Don't be afraid," he said, "Take courage! I am here!"

Reflection:

When you are in a scary situation, "Don't be afraid. Take courage! I am here!" Jesus will protect you.

When you are in serious trouble, "Don't be afraid. Take courage! I am here!" Jesus is in control.

Whenever you are struggling, "Don't be afraid. Take Courage! I am here!" Jesus will help you.

The One who walks on water will not walk by us, his followers, when we call to him in our time of need. He will get into the boat with us and calm the storm. And when we share the amazing things that Jesus has done for us with others, God will multiply our experience to meet the needs of many people.

MARK 7

Passage: Then he said, "You skillfully sidestep God's law in order to hold on to your own tradition."

Reflection:

The teachers of religious law and Pharisees were masters at sidestepping God's law to follow their own traditions. But, even today, some religions place traditions that are unbiblical above what God says in the Bible. They pray to people, they teach of a place between heaven and hell, and they say there is more than one way to heaven—to name a few.

In an effort to make themselves feel better, people sidestep the truth of God when they ignore what the Bible says to justify their own defiled lifestyle choices. Their hearts are far from God, and their worship is a farce.

MARK 8

Passage: Jesus turned around and looked at his disciples, then reprimanded Peter. "Get away from me, Satan!" he said. "You are seeing things merely from a human point of view, not from God's."

Reflection:

God looks at things from a spiritual and eternal point of view. But people often tend to focus on their physical and temporary circumstances. From God's point of view, there is nothing worth more than your soul. From a human point of view, suffering is a terrible thing. But what if suffering leads to the salvation of your soul? Then it is good.

This may not make sense to unbelievers because before we receive Jesus as our personal Savior, we are spiritually blind. But after we are born again, the Holy Spirit opens our spiritual eyes so we can clearly see and understand truth from God's point of view.

MARK 9

Passage: "Have mercy on us and help us, if you can."

Reflection:

"What do you mean, 'If I can'?"

Jesus was transformed, and his clothes became dazzling white.

"Anything is possible if a person believes."

A voice from the cloud said, "This is my dearly loved Son. Listen to him."

"What do you mean, 'If I can'?"

Jesus rebuked an evil spirit who then screamed, threw the boy into a violent convulsion, then left him.

"Anything is possible if a person believes."

Jesus said he would be betrayed into the hands of his enemies and killed, but three days later, he would rise from the dead.

"What do you mean, 'If I can'?"

People whose sins are not forgiven by Jesus will be thrown into the unquenchable fires of hell, where the maggots never die, and the fire never goes out.

MARK 10

Passage: "What do you want me to do for you?" Jesus asked.

Reflection:

Jesus is asking you this same question.

Do you want to inherit eternal life?

Do you want to enter the Kingdom of God?

Do you want to be forgiven for your sins?

Do you want to be healed?

Do you want to be free of fear, anxiety, shame, or guilt?

Do you want joy, peace, and purpose?

Do you want your entire life to be transformed?

Believe big and ask Jesus for whatever you want. It may seem impossible to you, but everything is possible with God!

MARK 11

Passage: Then Jesus said to the disciples, "Have faith in God."

Reflection:

With faith in God, believers in Jesus can command a mountain to move, and it will happen. When you have no doubt in your heart and really believe, you can pray for anything—and if you believe that you've received it, it will be yours. But even a little faith in a big God can result in amazing things.

The enemy of your soul wants you to focus on doubt and discouragement, but the Savior of your soul wants you to believe in him, who has been given all authority in heaven and earth, for great things. So pray to God with bold belief, knowing that our Father can and will answer the prayers of his children.

MARK 12

Passage: Jesus replied, "The most important commandment is this: 'Listen, O Israel! The Lord our God is the one and only Lord. And you must love the Lord your God with all your heart, all your soul, all your mind, and all your strength.' The second is equally important: 'Love your neighbor as yourself.' No other commandment is greater than these."

Reflection:

Did these people obey the most important commandment?

The religious leaders depicted as evil farmers who wanted to kill the Son of the Owner of the vineyard. No

The Pharisees who wanted to trap Jesus into saying something for which he could be arrested. No

The teacher of religious law who understood the most important commandment. Yes

The teachers of religious law who make long prayers in public but cheat widows out of their property. No

The widow who put everything she had to live on in the collection box at the Temple. Yes

Who do you love?

It is revealed in your heart, words, and actions. Jesus can see your heart, but others can hear what you say and see what you do.

MARK 13

Passage: "I say to you what I say to everyone: Watch for him!"

Reflection:

We don't know when Jesus will return—before dawn, at daybreak, in the evening, or at midnight—but we do know that he will return. Just as Jesus told Peter, James, John, and Andrew about the signs of his return, he has written them in the Bible to tell us. There will be false messiahs and false prophets, wars, famines, and earthquakes in increasing severity. Christians will be hated, arrested, and stand trial because they are followers of Jesus—but this is an opportunity to tell others about Jesus. It will be a terrible time of calamity and anguish.

When you see these things happening—as they already are—you can be sure that the return of Jesus is very near. And since no one except the Father knows when that time will come, may you not be found spiritually sleeping when Jesus arrives, but awake and watching for him with eager anticipation.

MARK 14

Passage: "Keep watch and pray, so that you will not give in to temptation. For the spirit is willing, but the body is weak."

Reflection:

Peter's spirit was willing to stay with Jesus, even through difficult times. But when Jesus was arrested, fear took over, and Peter, along with all the other disciples, deserted Jesus and ran away. The body is weak.

Peter's spirit was willing not to deny knowing Jesus, even if he had to die. But when people accused him of being one of Jesus' followers, fear took over, and Peter denied knowing Jesus three times. The body is weak.

We, as followers of Jesus, need to pray for strength in whatever challenges we are facing. Our spirit wants to do what is right and pleasing to God, but unless we pray like Jesus tells us, we will give in to temptation because the body is weak.

MARK 15

Passage: Then Jesus uttered another loud cry and breathed his last. And the curtain in the sanctuary of the Temple was torn in two, from top to bottom. When the Roman officer who stood facing him saw how he had died, he exclaimed, "This man truly was the Son of God!"

Reflection:

When Jesus Christ, the Son of God, died on the cross, God opened the barrier between him and people. This was symbolized by the curtain in the sanctuary of the Temple being torn from top to bottom. Because of Jesus' shed blood, the sins of those who ask him to be their Savior are forgiven. Because believers in Jesus are clean and holy in God's eyes, our Father in heaven encourages us to come directly and boldly to his throne of grace for anything—any day, anytime, anywhere.

MARK 16

Passage: And then he told them, "Go into all the world and preach the Good News to everyone. Anyone who believes and is baptized will be saved. But anyone who refuses to believe will be condemned."

Reflection:

Jesus rose from the dead!

The disciples didn't believe it at first when Mary Magdalene told them that Jesus was alive and that she had seen him.

Jesus rose from the dead!

The friends of two of his followers didn't believe it when they were told that Jesus appeared to them.

Jesus rose from the dead!

His eleven disciples finally believed after he appeared to them and rebuked them for their stubborn unbelief.

Do you believe that Jesus rose from the dead, was taken up into heaven, and is now sitting in the place of honor at God's right hand? Like the disciples, it may take you some time to accept this truth. But if—with God's help and faith—you believe, you will be saved from condemnation and have eternal life. Now go and tell the world the Good News!

✧ ✧ ✧

The Book of
LUKE

LUKE 1

Passage: "You are blessed because you believed that the Lord would do what he said."

Reflection:

When God sent the angel to Zechariah to tell him that his wife Elizabeth would become pregnant in her old age, he didn't believe what Gabriel said.

When God sent the angel Gabriel to Mary to tell her that she would give birth to the Son of God, she responded in faith, "I am the Lord's servant. May everything you have said about me come true."

Gabriel said, "For the word of God will never fail." Every word in the Bible is true, and everything that God tells us about the future will come true. How do you respond to Bible prophecy? Are you a doubter like Zechariah? Then, close your mouth until you can accept the truth. Or are you a believer like Mary? Then you are blessed—praise the Lord!

LUKE 2

Passage: Then Simeon blessed them, and he said to Mary, the baby's mother, "This child is destined to cause many in Israel to fall, but he will be a joy to many others. He has been sent as a sign from God, but many will oppose him."

Reflection:

The Savior of the world was born in Bethlehem, the City of David.

The Messiah was wrapped in strips of cloth, like a sacrificial lamb, and was lying in a manger.

The Lord's birth announcement was made by an angel who was joined by the angel armies of heaven in praising God.

God's salvation for all people had finally arrived.

He is a light to reveal God to the nations.

Jesus is his name.

LUKE 3

Passage: "Prove by the way you live that you have repented of your sins and turned to God. Don't just say to each other, 'We're safe, for we are descendants of Abraham.' That means nothing, for I tell you, God can create children of Abraham from these very stones."

Reflection:

No matter who you are, you must repent of your sins and be born again. Would God have given Jesus, his only Son, to die on the cross if it wasn't necessary to pay the penalty for sin?

No matter who your ancestors are, they cannot save you from hell. But those who belong to Jesus are safe and heaven bound.

No matter how "good" you are, you must accept God's gift of salvation through Jesus, his dearly loved Son, or be burned in a never-ending fire. But there is no condemnation for those who belong to Jesus.

LUKE 4

Passage: "He was led by the Spirit in the wilderness, where he was tempted by the devil for forty days."

Reflection:

In preparation for his ministry, the Holy Spirit led Jesus into the wilderness to fast and pray for forty days. But during that time he became very hungry. So, who showed up to tempt Jesus when he was in a vulnerable condition? The devil. The devil is the one who tempts you, too. He knows your weaknesses, and he will take advantage of your circumstances to get you to sin against God.

What can we do to have victory over temptation of any kind?

Pray. Jesus told Peter in Mark 14 to pray so that he would not give in to temptation because even though our spirit doesn't want to sin, our body is weak.

Quote Scripture. Jesus referred to actual passages in the Bible to combat the devil. The more you read the Bible, the more the Holy Spirit can bring truth to your mind. And if you can't remember a verse, search for the keyword in the Bible and read the verses. Reminding yourself of the truth will give you strength.

By imitating Jesus, we can win the spiritual battle of temptation and make the devil run.

LUKE 5

Passage: "Master," Simon replied, "we worked hard all last night and didn't catch a thing. But if you say so, I'll let the nets down again."

Reflection:

Simon and the other fishermen worked hard all night trying to catch fish. So when Jesus showed up on the shore of the Sea of Galilee and told them to go out in the deep water and let their nets down to catch some fish, Simon doubted that it would work. But even though he doubted, Simon did what Jesus told him to do. Not only did Simon's boat get filled with fish, but his partners' boat was filled too! The blessing Simon received for obedience spilled over onto those who were close to him.

Initially, Simon tried to catch fish in his own strength and caught nothing. But when he fished with the power of God, he caught boat loads of fish! Remember this the next time you go fishing—for fish or people!

LUKE 6

Passage: "But to you who are willing to listen, I say, love your enemies!"

Reflection:

How should children of the Most High treat people who are wicked?

With kindness.

How should followers of Jesus act toward people who are unthankful?

With compassion.

What did Jesus say to do to our enemies?

Love them.

How should we, who belong to God, behave towards people who hate us?

Do good to them.

When people curse believers in Jesus, how should we respond?

By blessing them.

When followers of Jesus Christ are hurt by others, what does our Lord want us to do?

Pray for them.

Christians will be excluded, mocked, and cursed as evil. But we can be happy because we have great blessings to look forward to. We can leap for joy because God has a great reward waiting for us in heaven!

LUKE 7

Passage: "Then she knelt behind him at his feet, weeping. Her tears fell on his feet, and she wiped them off with her hair. Then she kept kissing his feet and putting perfume on them."

Reflection:

When an immoral woman unexpectedly visited Jesus while he was at the home of Simon the Pharisee for dinner, Jesus fed him some truth.

Simon was indignant that Jesus would let a sinner, especially a woman, touch him. But Jesus answered his thoughts with a parable about forgiveness and love. Jesus pointed out the difference between little love shown to him by Simon the Pharisee and much love shown to him by the sinful woman.

For believers who have been saved by faith in Jesus, we have been forgiven of many sins. Let's show our gratitude to Jesus by kneeling at his feet—putting him first and obeying him. This is how we, like the sinful woman, can show him much love.

LUKE 8

Passage: "A farmer went out to plant his seed."

Reflection:

People respond to God's Word in four ways:

Some people who hear God's Word, cling to it, and patiently produce a huge harvest. These are the early bloomers.

Some people hear God's Word but do not believe or get saved because the devil takes it away from their hearts. These are the dormant, lifeless seeds.

Some people hear the message but never grow to maturity. They are too busy worrying about worldly things and chasing the pleasures and riches of this life. These seeds need guidance and encouragement.

Some people hear the message, receive it with joy, and believe for a while, but they fall away when they face temptation. These seeds need help.

So, according to the parable of the farmer scattering seed, approximately fifty percent of people who hear God's Word are late bloomers. That is why it's important for Christians to keep planting seeds and to help the struggling seeds take root and grow to maturity.

LUKE 9

Passage: "Come, follow me."

Reflection:

When Jesus invited a man to follow him, he replied, "Lord, first let me return home and bury my father."

Then, when another man was invited to follow Jesus, he responded, "Yes, Lord, I will follow you, but first let me say good-bye to my family."

When Jesus invites you to follow him, how will you respond? Will you put your family first, or will you put the Kingdom of God first? Will you look back at your life, your job, or the security you are leaving? Or will you obey Jesus and follow him—no ifs, ands, or buts?

LUKE 10

Passage: Jesus replied with a story: "A Jewish man was traveling from Jerusalem down to Jericho, and he was attacked by bandits. They stripped him of his clothes, beat him up, and left him half dead beside the road."

Reflection:

Based on the example of the Good Samaritan, this is how to love your neighbor:

He saw. Notice the people that God puts in your path who need help.

He felt compassion. Allow yourself to feel sympathy and concern for their suffering.

He went. Rather than walking by and going about your day, go to them.

He cared. Take care of their needs to the best of your ability. God will not lead you to someone that you cannot help.

He gave his money. Maybe the person has a need that can be met with physical things like money, food, clothing, or shelter. Be generous with what God has given you.

He gave his time. Often, people just need your time and a listening ear—someone to talk to and to show them the love and compassion of Jesus.

"Now go and do the same."

LUKE 11

Passage: "If you are filled with light, with no dark corners, then your whole life will be radiant, as though a floodlight were filling you with light."

Reflection:

When a person accepts Jesus into their heart to be their Savior, their sins are forgiven. At that moment, they receive the Holy Spirit of God, and they are filled with his pure, bright light.

Sin brings darkness into our lives. Even sin that is hidden in the dark corners, where no one else can see, can dim the light of the Holy Spirit. If we are careful to identify and repent of intentional and unintentional sin, then like being filled with the brightness of a floodlight, our whole life will shine radiantly!

LUKE 12

Passage: "Yes, a person is a fool to store up earthly wealth but not have a rich relationship with God."

Reflection:

Life is not measured by how much you own. Notice how many times the rich fool says the words "I" and "my":

What should *I* do?
I don't have...
My crops...
I know...
I'll tear down...
My barns...
I'll have...
My wheat...
I'll sit back...

This world tends to value self, things, accomplishment, and personal success. But people are the only things that will go on for eternity. So when we invest in a rich relationship with God and value people over possessions, we will store up treasures in heaven that last forever.

LUKE 13

Passage: "And you will perish, too, unless you repent of your sins and turn to God."

Reflection:

Many people try to enter God's Kingdom, but they will fail. They cannot go through the narrow door because they will not repent of their sins and turn to God. Jesus is the door to the Kingdom of Heaven, and those who refuse to invite him into their heart will not be known by God.

When we die, there are no more chances. It's too late—the narrow door to Heaven is locked. And those who do not know Jesus Christ as their Savior will be told, "I don't know you or where you came from. Get away from me, you who do evil." They will be thrown out to spend eternity where there is weeping and gnashing of teeth.

LUKE 14

Passage: "For those who exalt themselves will be humbled, and those who humble themselves will be exalted."

Reflection:

Unlike the guests who were all trying to sit in seats of honor at the dinner hosted by the leader of the Pharisees, as Christians, we should think of others as better than ourselves and be humble. Jesus humbled himself in obedience to God and came down from heaven to be born and die on the cross for us. Now, he is seated in the place of honor at God's right hand.

God opposes the proud and gives grace to the humble. So don't push for a place among the great. Don't exalt yourself. Wait for an invitation to the head of the table. Wait for God to honor you. For at just the right time, he will lift you up!

LUKE 15

Passage: "We had to celebrate this happy day."

Reflection:

When people try to find fulfillment by living like a prodigal, apart from God, they may eventually—by the grace of God—come to the end of themselves and come to their senses. God is watching and waiting to run to us, embrace us, and kiss us when we decide to return home to him.

There is more joy in heaven over one lost sheep who repents and returns to God than over ninety-nine others who are righteous and haven't strayed away. There is joy in the presence of God's angels when even one sinner repents. There is a celebration in heaven when the dead come back to life. Our heavenly Father throws a party when the lost sheep are found!

Oh, happy day!

LUKE 16

Passage: "If they won't listen to Moses and the prophets, they won't be persuaded even if someone rises from the dead."

Reflection:

In the Old Testament, Moses and the prophets talked about the coming Messiah—and the prophecies that pointed to the Messiah were fulfilled by Jesus Christ. But even though Jesus rose from the dead, just as he said he would, many people are not persuaded and refuse to believe in the Messiah. Sadly, unbelievers will not spend eternity with their beloved Abraham, who is with Jesus in heaven. They will spend eternity in the place of the dead where they will endure torment, anguish, and flames forever.

So choose wisely because the decision you make about Jesus during your lifetime will determine where you will spend eternity.

LUKE 17

Passage: "Has no one returned to give glory to God except this foreigner?"

Reflection:

Ten lepers cried out to Jesus to heal them. Ten lepers were healed. But only one, a Samaritan, returned to Jesus to thank him for what he had done.

This is probably still true today, where about ninety percent of people do not recognize or thank God regularly for the things he does for them. Has God provided food for you to eat today? Thank him. Has God prevented a close call from turning into an accident? Thank him. Has God healed you? Thank him. Did God answer a prayer? Thank him. Is your heart still beating? Thank him. Don't take the goodness of God for granted. Fall to your knees, thank him, and give him the glory he deserves for the things he does (and doesn't do) each day.

LUKE 18

Passage: "One day, Jesus told his disciples a story to show that they should always pray and never give up."

Reflection:

God invites his chosen people to wear him out with our constant prayer requests! He wants us to be persistent in our prayers. So, whether it's justice in a dispute with your enemy or something else, humbly cry out to God in prayer—day and night. Don't lose faith, and don't quit praying because your Father in heaven won't keep putting you off. Keep praying in the power of the Holy Spirit and trust in God's way and timing. He will answer your prayers when you least expect it. So never give up!

LUKE 19

Passage: "...you did not recognize it when God visited you."

Reflection:

When Jesus was born, so many people did not realize that he was God in the flesh.

When Jesus lived on earth and did miracles, most people did not accept that he was their long-awaited Messiah.

When Jesus rode through Jerusalem on a donkey's colt, the people did not understand that they were looking at the second person of the Trinity—God the Son.

When you read the Bible, do you realize that it is the living Word of God speaking directly to you?

When you feel convicted as you read, do you know that the Holy Spirit of God is urging you to repent and respond to what you hear or read?

As a child of God, do you have Spirit-eyes and Spirit-ears?

Are you attentive to his presence in every moment of your life?

Do you recognize it when God visits you?

LUKE 20

Passage: "Then Jesus was approached by some Sadducees—religious leaders who say there is no resurrection from the dead."

Reflection:

Whoever believes in Jesus becomes a child of God and a child of the resurrection. When we die, our body returns to the dust of the ground, but our spirit will return to God who gave it. In the age to come when Jesus returns, our bodies will be raised from the dead, and we will receive our heavenly bodies, never to die again.

Eternal life begins at the moment of salvation, and just as Jesus Christ was raised from the dead, so will we who belong to him be raised from the dead. Anyone who believes in Jesus will live, even after dying, for God is the God of the living, not the dead.

LUKE 21

Passage: "So when all these things begin to happen, stand and look up, for your salvation is near!"

Reflection:

Like the green leaves on a tree indicate that summer is near, these signs indicate that the Kingdom of God is near:

Persecution of Christians
False messiahs
Nations in turmoil
Wars
Earthquakes
Famines
Plagues
Roaring seas
Strange tides
Signs in the sun, moon, and stars

Then everyone will see the Son of Man coming on a cloud with power and great glory. So stay alert, be prepared, don't panic, and keep looking up because Jesus is about to make some noise!

LUKE 22

Passage: "Do this to remember me."

Reflection:

Before his suffering began, the last supper that Jesus ate with his disciples was the Passover meal. There, he thanked God for the bread and broke it in pieces explaining that it was his body, which was given for us. Jesus came down from his heavenly Kingdom to give his body on the cross for us.

Jesus also took a cup of wine and said that it was the new covenant between God and his people—an agreement confirmed with his blood, which was poured out as a sacrifice for us. The blood of Jesus was the complete and final sacrifice needed to forgive the sins of all people and bring us into a relationship with God.

When those who have accepted Jesus as their Savior and Lord take communion, we are remembering the precious sacrifice that Jesus gave for our eternal salvation—his body and his blood.

LUKE 23

Passage: "Father, forgive them, for they don't know what they are doing."

Reflection:

Even during the process of crucifixion, Jesus loved others. He loved others by speaking to the grief-stricken women as he was walking to the place of The Skull to be crucified. Jesus loved others by forgiving the people in the crowd, the soldiers, and the leaders who were demanding—and taking part in—his crucifixion. And Jesus loved others while he was hanging on the cross by giving salvation to the criminal hanging next to him, telling him, "Today you will be with me in paradise."

God showed how much he loves us by sending his one and only Son into the world so that we can have eternal life through him. This is real love.

LUKE 24

Passage: "Why are your hearts filled with doubt? Look at my hands. Look at my feet. You can see that it's really me. Touch me and make sure that I am not a ghost because ghosts don't have bodies, as you see that I do."

Reflection:

The Lord Jesus Christ is risen! He appeared to the two men walking to Emmaus, to his disciples, and to others after he rose from the dead. Our Savior is alive and well in heaven at this very moment. And he gives forgiveness of sins for all who repent.

Jesus was betrayed into the hands of sinful men, crucified, and rose again on the third day—just like the prophets wrote in Scripture. And in the same way he was taken up into heaven, the Messiah will return. Everything written about Jesus in the Bible must be fulfilled—and praise God—it will be!

✧ ✧ ✧

The Book of
JOHN

JOHN 1

Passage: "In the beginning, the Word already existed. The Word was with God, and the Word was God."

Reflection:

Jesus Christ, the Word, became human and made his home among us. The one and only Son of God gave up his glorious home in heaven and came down to earth as the sinless, spotless Lamb of God to take away the sins of the world.

Jesus, the Word, came into the very world he created, but the world didn't recognize him. Even his own people rejected him as the Chosen One of God. But only those who believe and accept Jesus are spiritually reborn and become children of God.

Jesus, the unique One, who is himself God, has revealed God to us. He gives us life, light, and blessing after blessing. He is full of unfailing love, faithfulness, and grace. And Jesus is the stairway between heaven and earth.

JOHN 2

Passage: But his mother told the servants, "Do whatever he tells you."

Reflection:

Just as Mary, the mother of Jesus, took the problem to him when the wine was gone, so should we take our problems to Jesus in faith—no matter how big or small they may seem. But it isn't enough to take our problems to the Lord. We must also do whatever he tells us.

We, as servants, must listen to Jesus and be filled like water jars with the living water of the Holy Spirit. We must read and follow the instructions of the Bible. And one day, as the bride of Christ, we will have a wedding celebration with Jesus that is out of this world. He is definitely keeping the best for last!

JOHN 3

Passage: "For this is how God loved the world. He gave his one and only Son so that everyone who believes in him will not perish but have eternal life."

Reflection:

Jesus came down from heaven to be lifted up on a cross so that everyone who believes in him will be born again and have eternal life. Without being born again of the Holy Spirit, we cannot see or enter the Kingdom of God.

God sent Jesus to save the world through him. The few who do what God wants—come to the light of Jesus and believe in him—will not suffer judgment. But the many who love darkness and do not come to Jesus, for fear their sins will be exposed, will never experience eternal life but will remain under God's angry judgment.

JOHN 4

Passage: Then Jesus told her, "I AM the Messiah!"

Reflection:

A Samaritan. A woman. A sinner. This was the first person that Jesus told directly that he is the Messiah.

On his way from Judea to Galilee, Jesus had to go through Samaria for a divine appointment with a woman at Jacob's well. This woman, who had been married five times and was currently living with a man, was a sinner and an outcast. Jesus told her that he could give her water that gives eternal life and becomes a fresh, bubbling spring within, so those who accept it will never be thirsty again. She believed him and said, "Give me this water."

The Samaritan woman, whose sins were forgiven, was bubbling with joy. She left her water jar beside the well, ran back to the village, and told everyone about Jesus! Many Samaritans believed in Jesus, the Savior of the world, because of what she told them. May we, as followers of Jesus, share the same joy and excitement as the Samaritan woman and tell others about the Messiah—because the fields are ripe for harvest.

Reading: JOHN 5

Passage: "You search the Scriptures because you think they give you eternal life. But the Scriptures point to me!"

Reflection:

The Old Testament Scriptures point to Jesus, the Messiah. So those who believe what Moses wrote should also believe in Jesus Christ, the One he wrote about.

Without believing in Jesus, the One God sent, you cannot hear God's voice or have his message in your heart. Without honoring Jesus, the Son of God, you cannot honor the Father who sent him. Without listening to the life-giving truth of the message of God and receiving his Son, you cannot have eternal life.

God the Father has given his Son absolute authority to judge. So anyone who accepts Jesus will never be condemned for their sins. They have passed from death to life. But those who reject the One God sent will one day experience the just judgment of the Son of God.

JOHN 6

Passage: Jesus told them, "This is the only work God wants from you: Believe in the One he has sent."

Reflection:

God the Father gave Jesus his seal of approval and sent him down from heaven to earth as the Bread of Life. Whoever comes to Jesus will never be hungry again. Whoever believes in Jesus will never be thirsty.

Through faith in Jesus, the Holy One of God, we are given eternal life. And those who believe will be raised on the last day. Anyone who spiritually eats the Bread from heaven will never die.

Jesus offered his own flesh and blood as a sacrifice on the cross so the world can receive forgiveness of sin and live. But some people will not believe. Only those whom God the Father has chosen to give to Jesus will believe and live forever.

JOHN 7

Passage: The people were surprised when they heard
him. "How does he know so much when he
hasn't been trained?" they asked.

Reflection:

In the Temple, Jesus proclaimed the message of God,
who sent him, to the people. He spoke the truth, not lies.
He spoke to honor his Father, not himself. Jesus foretold
his coming death when he said, "I will be with you only
a little while longer." He also spoke of his ascension back
to heaven when he said, "Then I will return to the one
who sent me."

Many among the crowds at the Temple did believe
in Jesus, but the Jewish leaders and Pharisees could not
understand what he meant. They searched the Scriptures
for signs of the Messiah, but they could not find him or
recognize him when he was standing right in front of
them. They were blind to what the Scriptures foretold
in passages such as Micah 5:2. They were trying to earn
righteousness by doing—following the law of Moses,
which none of them obeyed—rather than believing. But
without believing in Jesus Christ, people will not receive
the living water of the Holy Spirit, and they cannot go
to the Father where Jesus is.

JOHN 8

Passage: Jesus answered, "Since you don't know who I am, you don't know who my Father is. If you knew me, you would also know my Father."

Reflection:

"I tell you the truth."

If you don't know Jesus as your Savior, you don't know God. If you don't put your faith in Jesus, you will die in your sins. If you reject the Son of God, you can't enter heaven.

"I tell you the truth."

If you aren't from above, you are from below. If you don't belong to Jesus, God isn't your Father—the devil is. If the father of lies is your father, you hate the truth and don't believe it when you hear it. But if you belong to God, you gladly listen to the words of God.

"I tell you the truth."

If you aren't set free from sin by Jesus, you are a slave to sin. If you walk without Christ, you walk in darkness. But if you follow the Lord, you will have the light that leads to life.

JOHN 9

Passage: Then Jesus told him, "I entered this world to render judgment—to give sight to the blind and to show those who think they see that they are blind."

Reflection:

The man who was born blind was blind so the power of God could be seen in him. He was born to be healed by Jesus. He was given sight, so those who think they can see the things of God (like the Pharisees) could be shown how blind they really are.

"Ever since the world began, no one has been able to open the eyes of someone born blind." This healing was truly a miracle—we can't explain what Jesus did or how he did it—but the man went from blind to seeing. We are all born total sinners and spiritually blind, but those who go to Jesus, the Messiah sent by God, to have their sins washed away are declared not guilty by God. We can't explain what God does or how he does it—because salvation is a miracle. We only need to believe in the Lord Jesus Christ.

Can you see?

JOHN 10

Passage: "I am the good shepherd."

Reflection:

Jesus is the good shepherd of his sheep. He calls his sheep by name. He leads them, walking ahead of them. The sheep who belong to Jesus know his voice and follow him. Those who do not believe in Jesus do not belong to him or God the Father—because the Son and the Father are one. And there is only one flock, one gate, and one shepherd.

The purpose of the thief—the devil—is to steal your freedom and joy, kill your soul, and destroy your life. But Jesus gives his sheep good pastures, freedom from sin, and a rich and satisfying life. Jesus, the good shepherd, voluntarily sacrificed his life for the sheep. He gives them eternal life, and they will never perish. And no one can ever snatch Jesus' sheep away from him.

JOHN 11

Passage: Jesus told her, "I am the resurrection and the life. Anyone who believes in me will live, even after dying. Everyone who lives in me and believes in me will never die."

Reflection:

Lazarus, a dear friend of Jesus, became sick and died for the glory of God. Jesus purposefully waited until Lazarus died before going to Bethany so that the Son of God would receive glory from his resurrection. And sure enough when Jesus shouted, "Lazarus, come out!" He came out of the tomb wrapped in grave clothes!

Because Jesus holds the keys of death and the grave, the bodies of believers, which lie dead and buried, will one day rise to everlasting life. As Isaiah prophesied, "But those who die in the Lord will live; their bodies will rise again! Those who sleep in the earth will rise up and sing for joy! For your life-giving light will fall like dew on your people in the place of the dead!"

JOHN 12

Passage: Jesus shouted to the crowds, "If you trust me, you are trusting not only me but also God who sent me. For when you see me, you are seeing the one who sent me. I have come as a light to shine in this dark world so that all who put their trust in me will no longer remain in the dark."

Reflection:

Mary received the light of Jesus and let it shine in her life. She anointed his feet with twelve ounces of expensive perfume and wiped them with her hair. The house was filled with the fragrance of her love for Jesus.

Some of the Jewish leaders received the light of Jesus, but they kept it hidden. They believed in Jesus, but they wouldn't admit it because they were afraid of being expelled from the synagogue. They loved human praise more than the praise of God.

Most of the people rejected the light of the Messiah—just as Isaiah prophesied. They refused to believe in Jesus. Their eyes were blind, and they walked in darkness, unable to see where they were going. Their hearts were hard, unable to understand. They and anyone who rejects Jesus and his message will be judged on Judgment Day.

Which of these can you identify with?

JOHN 13

Passage: Jesus replied, "Unless I wash you, you won't belong to me."

Reflection:

When people accept Jesus as their Savior, they are spiritually washed clean—from head to toe. The filth of their sin is gone. They receive a new heart that is tender and responsive. And they are given a new spirit that follows the Lord and obeys him.

But even after we receive God's gift of salvation, we still live in human bodies with a sinful nature. As we walk in this world, our feet become dirty with sinful thoughts, words, and actions. So we, like Jesus did for his disciples, must wash away the dirt of our daily sin through repentance. This will make us entirely clean and allow us to stay in close fellowship with the Lord.

JOHN 14

Passage: Jesus told him, "I am the way, the truth, and the life. No one can come to the Father except through me."

Reflection:

The truth is that no one can enter the Father's home except through Jesus, the only way to God. Just believe in Jesus with the faith of a child, and the Holy Spirit of God will be given to you. He will never abandon you. He will lead you into all truth. He will teach you. And he will remind you of what Jesus said.

Jesus gives all who believe in him and belong to him a gift that the world cannot give—peace of mind and heart. We also have the assurance of his constant presence through the Holy Spirit. And since Jesus lives, we have the promise of eternal life. In addition, we have the guarantee that when everything is ready, Jesus will come again to get us, and we will always be with him in the Father's home. So don't be troubled or afraid.

JOHN 15

Passage: "Remain in me, and I will remain in you."

Reflection:

Remain. Jesus used this word ten times when he spoke about the Vine and the branches. If we remain in Jesus, we can be fruitful. If we remain in Jesus, we can ask for anything in his name, and the Father will give it to us. But if we do not remain in the Vine, we can do nothing. We become like a useless, withering branch.

How do we remain in Jesus? By obeying his commands. This is his command: Love each other. Jesus demonstrated the greatest form of love when he obeyed the Father and sacrificed his life for us. And the result—overflowing joy!

Remain in Jesus. Obey God. Love each other. Be filled with joy.

JOHN 16

Passage: "Here on earth, you will have many trials and sorrows. But take heart, because I have overcome the world."

Reflection:

Jesus warned us that the time would come, and it is here now, when those who kill Christians think they are doing a holy service for God. The truth is, they have never known God the Father or God the Son. And that is the world's sin—refusal to believe in Jesus Christ.

Christians will have grief while living in this world, but one day, we will see Jesus. Our sorrow and anguish will turn to wonderful joy! Until then, we have the Advocate with us, the Holy Spirit of truth, who tells us whatever he receives from Jesus. So don't be shaken, we are not alone. The Overcomer is on our side!

JOHN 17

Passage: "I am praying not only for these disciples but also for all who will ever believe in me through their message."

Reflection:

Jesus prayed to his Father in heaven for all people who have been given to him—those who have accepted that Jesus came from God and believed in him. Jesus prayed for the Father to protect us by the power of his name and keep us safe from the evil one. He prayed that we would be united as Jesus and the Father are united. Jesus also prayed that God would teach us and make us holy by his Word, which is truth. And Jesus prayed that all who have been given to him will be with him where he is, so we can see all the glory he shared with the Father even before the world began!

Jesus, thank you for your loving prayer. Thank you for giving yourself as a holy sacrifice for us so we can be made holy. And thank you for giving us eternal life so we can be with you where you are forever. Amen.

JOHN 18

Passage: "Shall I not drink from the cup of suffering the Father has given me?"

Reflection:

Even Jesus, God's one and only Son, was given a cup of suffering from his Father. But even though he knew exactly what was in the cup, he still agreed to drink it because of his love for his Father, his love for sinful people, and the glory that awaited him.

God has also planned events in our lives that bring suffering. We don't usually get to know ahead of time what is in our cup because rather than agreeing to drink it, we would push it away. Many times we question the Father's love when we suffer, but even when times are hard, God's plan is still good, and he still loves us. Whether we suffer like Jesus—abandonment, betrayal, false accusations, beating—or in a different way, God gives us the grace we need to endure. Remember this: What we suffer now is nothing compared to the glory he will reveal to us later.

JOHN 19

Passage: Jesus knew his mission was now finished, and to fulfill Scripture, he said, "I am thirsty." A jar of sour wine was sitting there, so they soaked a sponge in it, put it on a hyssop branch, and held it up to his lips. When Jesus had tasted it, he said, "It is finished!" Then he bowed his head and released his spirit.

Reflection:

Jesus came down from heaven to fulfill a mission for God. That mission was to sacrifice himself on the cross to pay for the sins of all people. Without the sacrifice of Jesus, the sinless Lamb of God, we would all be doomed to an eternity in hell because we can't be sinless. There is nothing we can do on our own—no number of good deeds—to earn our way into heaven.

Jesus finished the mission that God sent him to do. Now, it is up to you to decide for yourself whether to accept his payment for all your sins or whether you will try to do the impossible and pay for them on your own. Jesus suffered on the cross, so you won't have to suffer for eternity. He is the only way to God. He is the only way to eternal life. Choose wisely.

JOHN 20

Passage: "The disciples saw Jesus do many other miraculous signs in addition to the ones recorded in this book. But these are written so that you may continue to believe that Jesus is the Messiah, the Son of God, and that by believing in him, you will have life by the power of his name."

Reflection:

Jesus did many miracles, but his resurrection from the dead is the miracle that proves that we who believe in him are forgiven for our sins and will also be resurrected. This miracle helps believers know that we have eternal life after death.

Blessed are those who believe in Jesus, the Messiah, by faith.

Blessed are those who love Jesus, the Son of God, even though they have never seen him.

Blessed are those who trust the Lord. Their reward is the Holy Spirit of peace and eternal life by the power of the name of Jesus.

JOHN 21

Passage: "Simon, son of John, do you love me?"

Reflection:

   Jesus asked Simon Peter if he loved him three times. After each question, Peter answered, "Yes, Lord, you know I love you." But Jesus took it a step further and told Peter to feed and take care of his lambs and sheep. This is how we show our love for Jesus—by loving others.

   Jesus then told Peter, "Follow me." To follow the Lord, we must give up our own way, our own understanding, and trust Jesus to show us which path to take. Because when we try to do things on our own, it's like fishing all night and ending up with nothing to show for our efforts. But when we follow Jesus and obey him, our net will be overflowing with fish!

✧ ✧ ✧

The Book of
ACTS

ACTS 1

Passage: "During the forty days after he suffered and died, he appeared to the apostles from time to time, and he proved to them in many ways that he was actually alive. And he talked to them about the Kingdom of God."

Reflection:

Jesus is alive! Our God is not dead. He is in heaven, this very moment, ruling and reigning over every detail of your life and the universe he created. One day, he will descend from heaven in the same way he ascended.

Until Jesus returns (only God knows the date and time when that will happen), we who have received the Holy Spirit are his witnesses. Our assignment from the Lord is to tell people about him everywhere—starting with our own home and expanding out to the ends of the earth. So let's think outside the box for creative ways of telling others about our Savior, Jesus Christ.

ACTS 2

Passage: "Each of you must repent of your sins and turn to God, and be baptized in the name of Jesus Christ for the forgiveness of your sins. Then, you will receive the gift of the Holy Spirit."

Reflection:

The Holy Spirit initially filled all the believers on the day of Pentecost. Since then, people who repent and turn to God by calling on the name of Jesus will be saved and receive the gift of the Holy Spirit—the third person of the Trinity.

After salvation, Christians should follow the pattern of early believers by devoting themselves to teaching, prayer, worship, and fellowship. This is the way of life that is superior to the rest of the world: being filled with the Holy Spirit and living each day in the joy of God's presence.

ACTS 3

Passage: But Peter said, "I don't have any silver or gold for you. But I'll give you what I have. In the name of Jesus Christ, the Nazarene, get up and walk!"

Reflection:

Moses told the people of Israel that God would raise up a Prophet from among his own people and warned them to listen carefully to everything he told them. But in their ignorance, the people rejected Jesus, the Messiah appointed by God, and handed him over to be crucified. Rather than accept the holy, righteous one of God, they killed him. But God raised the author of life from the dead!

A relationship with Jesus cannot be purchased with silver or gold but can only be received through faith, like that of the lame man. Those who will not accept Jesus will be completely cut off from God. But those who believe, repent of their sins, and turn to God will have their sins wiped away. They will be blessed, refreshed, and will jump for joy, especially when Jesus comes again for the final restoration of all things. Hallelujah!

ACTS 4

Passage: "And now, O Lord, hear their threats, and give us, your servants, great boldness in preaching your word."

Reflection:

Peter and John were ordinary men with no special training in the Scriptures, but they had great boldness as they taught the people that through Jesus, there is resurrection of the dead. The Holy Spirit filled Peter with great boldness when he told the council that the lame man was healed by the powerful name of Jesus Christ—the man they crucified but whom God raised from the dead. And that there is salvation in no one else because God has given no other name under heaven by which we must be saved!

May Christians today have the same courage as Peter and John to obey God and not stop telling others about Jesus. And may we preach the Word with great boldness despite the threats of those who are united against God's anointed.

Reading: **ACTS 5**

Passage: The apostles left the high council rejoicing that God had counted them worthy to suffer disgrace for the name of Jesus. And every day, in the Temple and from house to house, they continued to teach and preach this message: "Jesus is the Messiah."

Reflection:

After the angel of the Lord opened the gates of the jail and set the apostles free, they entered the Temple at daybreak and immediately started teaching again! Even though the authorities warned them never to teach in Jesus' name, they had to obey God. The high council wanted to kill them, but they accepted the advice of Gamaliel, had them flogged, gave them another warning, and let them go.

Even today, people try to eliminate Jesus from the world—but God's plans cannot be overthrown. Do not fear because the battle is not yours. They are fighting against God!

ACTS 6

Passage: "At this point, everyone in the high council stared at Stephen, because his face became as bright as an angel's."

Reflection:

Stephen was a man full of faith and the Holy Spirit. He was also a man full of God's grace and power, who did amazing miracles and signs among the people.

Stephen spoke with wisdom from the Holy Spirit, so is it any wonder that the men from the synagogue couldn't stand him? Their jealousy led to persuading people to lie and be false witnesses against Stephen. And just like Jesus, he was brought before the high council. But Stephen was not alone. The presence of Christ in him was so powerful that it illuminated his face, and everyone stared at him! If this was the measure of your faith and fellowship with Jesus, how bright would your face shine? Would citizens stop and stare at you? Would passers-by pause and glimpse at you? Or would walkers keep on walking, hardly noticing anything unusual?

ACTS 7

Passage: "Lord Jesus, receive my spirit."

Reflection:

As Stephen pointed out how the Israelites persecuted and even killed the prophets of God who predicted the coming of the Messiah (who they betrayed and murdered), he looked up and saw Jesus in heaven standing in the place of honor at God's right hand. Even as Stephen was being stoned to death, he forgave his accusers and asked the Lord not to charge them for their sin.

Stephen's words still ring true today: "You stubborn people! You are heathen at heart and deaf to the truth. Must you forever resist the Holy Spirit?"

God will not receive the spirit of those who resist the Holy Spirit and reject Jesus Christ, the Righteous One. When they die, their spirit will not go to a place of rest like Stephen's, but instead, their spirit will go to a place of suffering and be forever separated from God and his love.

ACTS 8

Passage: Philip ran over and heard the man reading from the prophet Isaiah. Philip asked, "Do you understand what you are reading?" The man replied, "How can I unless someone instructs me?"

Reflection:

The Lord knew that the treasurer of Ethiopia was reading Scripture and needed help to understand it, so he sent Philip to teach him. In the same way, God knows that we need help to understand the Bible, so he gave us teachers, preachers, and the Holy Spirit. The Scriptures point to Jesus, so as you read them, look for Jesus on every page. Philip was able to tell the Ethiopian the Good News by explaining that Isaiah was talking about Jesus, who was led like a sheep to the slaughter.

Reading, understanding, and obeying the Bible results in salvation for those who believe with all their heart that Jesus Christ is the Son of God. And those who do accept God's gift will have eternal life and go on their way rejoicing as a child of God!

ACTS 9

Passage: "Meanwhile, Saul was uttering threats with every breath and was eager to kill the Lord's followers."

Reflection:

Saul was chosen by God to take the message of Jesus to the Gentiles, and his salvation experience was truly amazing. He went from persecutor to preacher in just a few days! But as his preaching and proof that Jesus is the Messiah became more powerful, so did the threats against his life. Jesus had told Ananias, "I will show him how much he must suffer for my name's sake." And as some believers helped Saul escape by lowering him in a basket through an opening in the city wall, this was only the beginning.

When a person suddenly hears the voice of the Lord Jesus, as Saul did, they are shocked and speechless. Pride and arrogance are quickly replaced with the fear of God and humble obedience. When Jesus says, "Now get up and go and you will be told what you must do." You will say, "Yes, Lord!"

ACTS 10

Passage: ... "Jesus is the one appointed by God to be the judge of all—the living and the dead. He is the one all the prophets testified about, saying that everyone who believes in him will have their sins forgiven through his name."

Reflection:

Everyone means all people. No one is excluded from believing in Jesus and having their sins forgiven. God made it clear to Peter, by calling all different kinds of animals clean, that he shows no favoritism. People of every nation, skin color, and ethnicity are accepted by God when they fear him and do what is right—believe in his Son, Jesus Christ, for the forgiveness of their sins. Everyone can have peace with God through Jesus, who is the Lord of all. Everyone who receives Jesus as their Savior also receives the Holy Spirit. And everyone who receives the Holy Spirit can be baptized.

ACTS 11

Passage: "God has also given the Gentiles the privilege
of repenting of their sins and receiving eternal
life."

Reflection:

Who are we to stand in God's way? Who are we to create barriers for people who want to repent of their sins? Who are we to determine who can receive eternal life?

Because some of the believers went to Antioch after Stephen's death and began preaching to the Gentiles, a large number of Gentiles believed and turned to the Lord. It was there, at Antioch, that the believers were first called Christians.

And because Jewish believers did not let their initial objections stand in the way of God's plan, the brothers and sisters in Jerusalem were blessed by the relief sent to them from Christians in Antioch. May we not stand in the way of God's plans. If we do, who knows what blessings we may be preventing for ourselves and others.

ACTS 12

Passage: "But while Peter was in prison, the church prayed very earnestly for him."

Reflection:

What can the power of prayer do? Send an angel of the Lord to a prison cell. Make a prisoner's chains fall off while he lay between two soldiers. Enable the prisoner to walk past, not one—but two, guard posts. And make the iron gate to the city swing open on its own! Can you imagine Peter's surprise and joy when this happened to him?

James 5:16 says: "The earnest prayer of a righteous person has great power and produces wonderful results." And here is a perfect example of that truth—the church prayed very earnestly, and the Lord Jesus sent his angel to rescue Peter. So don't underestimate the incredible greatness of God's power in response to earnest prayer. Who knows, the chains that are broken may be yours, and the prisoner who is set free may be you!

ACTS 13

Passage: Then Paul and Barnabas spoke out boldly and declared, "It was necessary that we first preach the Word of God to you Jews. But since you have rejected it and judged yourselves unworthy of eternal life, we will offer it to the Gentiles."

Reflection:

The law of Moses could never make a person right with God. But it is great for showing a person how sinful they are and how much they need a Savior. Jesus is the one who forgives sin, and everyone who believes in Jesus is made right with God.

Those who reject Jesus are judging themselves unworthy of eternal life. They will be rejected by God as enemies of all that is good, and the Lord will lay his hand of punishment on them. But all who are chosen for eternal life will become believers who are filled with joy and the Holy Spirit.

ACTS 14

Passage: "We have come to bring you the Good News that you should turn from these worthless things and turn to the living God, who made heaven and earth, the sea, and everything in them."

Reflection:

Paul and Barnabas preached boldly with the power of the Holy Spirit, and many Jews and Greeks became believers. The Lord even proved their message was true by giving them power to do miraculous signs and wonders, like healing a man who was crippled from birth. Even though Paul was stoned—almost to death— he didn't quit. He got up and kept going!

As believers, we should be strengthened by the experiences of Paul and Barnabas. We should be encouraged as we read about how God, in his grace, opened doors of opportunity for them. And we should continue in the faith, even though we suffer hardships. Then, at the end of our journey, we will have completed the work entrusted to us, and we can gladly celebrate everything that God has done!

ACTS 15

Passage: "We believe that we are all saved the same way, by the undeserved grace of the Lord Jesus."

Reflection:

Whether Jew or Gentile, it is not following the law of Moses that saves you. Just as Peter told the apostles and elders, people are saved by grace alone, through faith alone, in Christ alone. So when someone tries to burden you with another rule you must follow or thing you must do to be saved, don't believe them.

Christians should always look to God's Word for the truth. We should listen to regular teaching and preaching of the Bible so our faith will be strengthened. We should also gather with other believers so we can support and encourage each other. And as we travel through life, may God's true children be blessed with peace as we trust in the Lord's gracious care.

ACTS 16

Passage: The jailer called for lights and ran to the dungeon and fell down, trembling before Paul and Silas. Then he brought them out and asked, "Sirs, what must I do to be saved?"

Reflection:

Sometimes, we will encounter resistance and persecution, even when we are obeying the will of God—just as Paul and Silas did in Philippi. After commanding a demon to come out of a girl, they were dragged before the authorities, beaten with wooden rods, and put in prison. But what did Paul and Silas do? They made the best of their situation by praying and singing hymns to God as the other prisoners listened—and no doubt those prisoners believed in Jesus because of what they heard. Then God sent a massive earthquake, the prison doors flew open, and the chains fell off every prisoner! As a result, even the jailer and his household were saved! The Holy Spirit sends Christians wherever there are people who need to be freed from their chains of sin—it could even mean going to prison for Jesus.

ACTS 17

Passage: "God overlooked people's ignorance about these things in the past, but now he commands everyone everywhere to repent of their sins and turn to him."

Reflection:

God made the world and everything in it. God has no needs but satisfies every need. And as God's created offspring, we live because he has given us life. God has also appointed his Son, Jesus Christ, whom he raised from the dead, to judge the sins of the world—everyone, everywhere. But because of God's great love, he offers us the gift of salvation when we repent of our sins and turn to him.

God is not far from anyone. He listens to your words. He hears your thoughts. He knows your heart. So P-R-A-Y to God every day: praise him, repent of your sins, ask him for what you need, and yield to God's will. Then you will be holy and without fault as you live and move and exist in him for eternity.

ACTS 18

Passage: One night, the Lord spoke to Paul in a vision and told him, "Don't be afraid! Speak out! Don't be silent! For I am with you, and no one will attack and harm you, for many people in this city belong to me."

Reflection:

When you, as a follower of Jesus, speak out and testify about the truth of Scripture, some people will oppose and insult you. But don't worry, just walk away. Their blood is on their own heads.

After you experience rejection, it's tempting to quit. But don't be afraid and don't keep silent. Jesus is with you and wants you to continue to speak out with an enthusiastic spirit. And God willing, may you have many occasions where you will be welcomed, people will receive your message, Christians will be strengthened by your teaching of the Word, and the unsaved will become believers in Jesus.

ACTS 19

Passage: But this time, when they tried it, the evil spirit
             replied, "I know Jesus, and I know Paul, but
             who are you?"

Reflection:

Satan knows Jesus, is threatened by him, and will try anything to stop believers from spreading the Good News. One of Satan's tactics is to deceive people from knowing Jesus by getting them to worship idols instead of God. Idols can be wealth, power, or man-made shrines such as the goddess Artemis—anything other than the One True God.

When the message of Jesus causes a solemn fear and people confess and turn from their sinful ways, Satan strikes back at Jesus by attacking Christians. As happened in the amphitheater in Ephesus, Satan loves to stoke the fire to incite people to anger. He is happy when people are shouting, confused, and rioting—even if some of the people participating don't have a clue about why they are there! When evil rages, Jesus is still Prince of Peace.

ACTS 20

Passage: "But my life is worth nothing to me unless I use it for finishing the work assigned me by the Lord Jesus—the work of telling others the Good News about the wonderful grace of God."

Reflection:

There is one message for everyone—repent of your sin and turn to God through faith in the Lord Jesus Christ. This is the Good News of salvation. Because of God's wonderful grace, he will forgive us of our sins—past, present, and future—when we repent and receive Jesus as our Savior and Lord. You do not have to suffer eternal death in hell, but you can be assured of eternal life in heaven when you become a child of God.

Today, we are surrounded by false teachers who, like vicious wolves, are distorting the truth of the Bible. Beware! They are teaching that what is wrong is right and what is right is wrong. Watch out! They are also teaching that God's grace is not enough to be made right with him and to inherit the Kingdom of God. Don't believe them! Guard your heart and mind and believe God's Word and the Holy Spirit, who will guide you into all truth.

ACTS 21

Passage: Several days later, a man named Agabus, who also had the gift of prophecy, arrived from Judea. He came over, took Paul's belt, and bound his own feet and hands with it. Then he said, "The Holy Spirit declares, 'So shall the owner of this belt be bound by the Jewish leaders in Jerusalem and turned over to the Gentiles.'"

Reflection:

Paul was warned of what was going to happen to him in Jerusalem, but it didn't stop him from going there. He was ready to go to jail and even die for the Lord Jesus. And just as Paul was warned, a mob was roused against him, which turned into a riot. The people were trying to kill Paul, but God rescued him through Roman soldiers who bound him with two chains and ordered him to be taken to the fortress.

Paul entrusted his life to Jesus, and God was his fortress. He continued to follow the Holy Spirit's leading, knowing that he was never alone and that nothing could happen to him outside of the will of God. May you, like Paul, be so surrendered to Jesus that you are able to say of your own life, "The Lord's will be done."

ACTS 22

Passage: "Then he told me, 'The God of our ancestors has chosen you to know his will and to see the Righteous One and hear him speak. For you are to be his witness, telling everyone what you have seen and heard. What are you waiting for?'"

Reflection:

Paul was chosen by God to be his witness and to tell everyone about Jesus—and that is exactly what he was doing in Jerusalem when he was arrested. Paul was giving his testimony. He told the people about his past and how he used to be. He told them how he came to know Jesus Christ as his Savior and the difference Jesus made in his life. And Paul told those listening to him that they must call on the name of Jesus to have their sins washed away.

As a born again Christian, it was God's will that you were chosen to have your sins washed away and become a follower of Jesus. Because of this, you are also chosen to be a witness for him, telling everyone what you have experienced in Christ. What are you waiting for?

ACTS 23

Passage: That night, the Lord appeared to Paul and said, "Be encouraged, Paul. Just as you have been a witness to me here in Jerusalem, you must preach the Good News in Rome as well."

Reflection:

God rescued Paul again. He made the soldiers take him out of the violent high council meeting and take him back to the fortress where he was safe. God also made sure that Paul's nephew overheard an oath made by more than forty Jews to kill Paul. So he avoided that too, with the help of the commander who sent him safely to Caesarea—just where Jesus wanted him to go. While there, Paul would be given an opportunity to preach the Good News to Governor Felix!

Paul was moved from the fortress to prison at Herod's headquarters. These were probably not comfortable places to stay, but Paul was safe. Christians, like Paul, are not only given the privilege of trusting in Christ, but we are also given the privilege of suffering for him as we preach the Good News wherever he sends us.

ACTS 24

Passage: "We have found this man to be a troublemaker who is constantly stirring up riots among the Jews all over the world. He is a ringleader of the cult known as the Nazarenes."

Reflection:

Satan is known as the Accuser. He loves to falsely accuse believers in Jesus of doing evil. Paul was accused of being a troublemaker, but he was never found arguing. He was accused of constantly stirring up riots, but his accusers couldn't prove that either. He was a follower of the Way, which Tertullus, the lawyer for the Jews, accused of being a cult.

When unbelievers become threatened, frightened, convicted, or uncomfortable with the truth of the Bible, they conveniently label it as hate speech and accuse God, its Author, of being intolerant. In fact, what they are really saying to God is, "Go away! Maybe when I'm at the end of myself and desperate, I'll call for you again."

ACTS 25

Passage: Paul denied the charges. "I am not guilty of any crime against the Jewish laws or the Temple or the Roman government," he said.

Reflection:

The Jewish leaders wanted to convict Paul without a trial, but Festus gave him the chance to confront his accusers and defend himself. The Jewish elders made many serious accusations against Paul, which they couldn't prove. Paul was not guilty of harming the Jews. He had done nothing deserving of the death penalty. And there was no clear charge against him. But he did talk about Jesus and how he is not dead, but alive!

Behind the false accusations, behind the hearts of the Jewish priests and leaders, was Satan. Spiritual warfare is something we can't see, and many people don't comprehend, but it is the root cause of many conflicts. Followers of Jesus understand that we are not fighting against people made of flesh and blood but against evil authorities of the dark and unseen world. May we stand firm against evil and be strong in our faith and in the mighty power of the Lord Jesus Christ.

ACTS 26

Passage: "I teach nothing except what the prophets and Moses said would happen—that the Messiah would suffer and be the first to rise from the dead, and in this way announce God's light to the Jews and Gentiles alike."

Reflection:

Prior to his encounter with Jesus on the road to Damascus, Paul did everything he could to oppose Jesus and his followers. He punished them in synagogues, trying to get them to curse Jesus. He chased them down in foreign cities. He caused many believers to be sent to prison. And he voted for them to be condemned to death. Now Paul was the one on trial for Jesus. Why? Because he proclaimed that God's promise of a Messiah and a Light for all people was fulfilled in Jesus.

What was Paul's message that was so threatening to Satan? The same gospel message that Christians preach today: Turn from darkness to light and from the power of Satan to God. Then, you will receive forgiveness for your sins and be given a place among God's people, who are set apart by faith in Jesus.

ACTS 27

Passage: "For last night, an angel of the God to whom I belong and whom I serve stood beside me, and he said, 'Don't be afraid, Paul, for you will surely stand trial before Caesar! What's more, God in his goodness has granted safety to everyone sailing with you.' So take courage! For I believe God. It will be just as he said."

Reflection:

Slow sailing, great difficulty, against the wind, struggle, dangerous, terrible storm, gale-force winds, all hope was gone! Does this sometimes sound like your life? Being a follower of Jesus doesn't exempt us from storms, but it gives us someone to go to when they come. Jesus will speak into our storm, "Peace, be still!"

So when we struggle and reach a point where it seems like all hope is gone, may we trust God and believe his Word. Because our God is faithful, and he will do just as he said.

ACTS 28

Passage: "He explained and testified about the Kingdom of God and tried to persuade them about Jesus from the Scriptures."

Reflection:

The Messiah—the hope of Israel—has already come! That belief is why Paul was bound with chains. But no matter where he went, even the island of Malta, Paul testified about Jesus with his words and deeds. Some people believed the message of salvation through Jesus, but others could not comprehend what Paul said because their hearts were hardened.

Dear Heavenly Father,

With my words and deeds, help me to boldly proclaim the Kingdom of God and teach the people you lead to me about the Lord Jesus Christ.

In Jesus's name,
Amen.

✧ ✧ ✧

The Book of
ROMANS

ROMANS 1

Passage: "Since they thought it foolish to acknowledge God, he abandoned them to their foolish thinking and let them do things that should never be done."

Reflection:

Through creation, God made his invisible qualities clear and obvious, so people have no excuse for not knowing God. But dark and wicked minds will not worship the glorious and eternal God. As a result, God abandons them to their shameful desires, which include women turning against the natural way to have sex and having sex with each other, and men burning with lust for each other and doing shameful things with other men. These acts are not normal or natural, and God calls it sin. God's justice requires that people who sin deserve the penalty for sin, which is eternal death.

From pride to perversion and greed to gossip, everyone has sinned. But thank God for the Good News, which tells us all how we can be made right in God's sight! It is accomplished from start to finish by faith in Jesus Christ, the Son of God, who was raised from the dead. Everyone who believes and receives Jesus by faith is saved from the penalty of sin, is made righteous in God's eyes, and has eternal life.

ROMANS 2

Passage: "And this is the message I proclaim—that the day is coming when God, through Christ Jesus, will judge everyone's secret life."

Reflection:

A day is coming when God will judge everyone for what they have done. He will give eternal life to people who seek after the immortality that is offered through Jesus Christ. But God will pour out his anger and wrath on people who live lives of wickedness and refuse to act on the truth of the Bible. There will be glory, honor, and peace from God for all who do good. But there will be trouble, calamity, and terrible punishment for all who keep doing what is evil and stubbornly refuse to turn from sin.

Don't just listen to what the Bible says—that does not make you right with God. Obey and do what God's Word says, making Jesus your Savior and letting the Holy Spirit change your heart, then you will truly be a child of God who is made right in his sight.

ROMANS 3

Passage: "We are made right with God by placing our faith in Jesus Christ. And this is true for everyone who believes, no matter who we are."

Reflection:

We are not made right with God by obeying the Ten Commandments—it's impossible! They were given to us to show us how sinful we are, and that the entire world is guilty before God because the entire world is under the power of sin.

But God doesn't just point out our sinfulness. He also has shown us how to be made right with him. By placing our faith in Jesus Christ and believing that he sacrificed his life and shed his blood, we sinners are declared right in God's sight.

"There is only one God, and he makes people right with himself only by faith."

ROMANS 4

Passage: "But people are counted as righteous, not because of their work, but because of their faith in God who forgives sinners."

Reflection:

As Abraham waited for God to fulfill his promise of a son, even though he was 100 years old when it happened, his faith never wavered—it grew stronger! He was fully convinced that if God could bring the dead back to life and create new things out of nothing, then he could certainly create life in Sarah's womb, no matter how old she was.

Abraham was counted as righteous by God because of his faith. And he is the spiritual father of all who have a right relationship with God by faith. Abraham believed in God, and he is the father of all who believe in Jesus—whether Jew or Gentile.

God will count us as righteous if we believe in Jesus—

The One who was handed over to die because of our sins,

The One who God raised from the dead,

The One who makes us right with God.

ROMANS 5

Passage: "When Adam sinned, sin entered the world. Adam's sin brought death, so death spread to everyone, for everyone sinned."

Reflection:

The sin of Adam brought death to many.

But receiving God's gift through Jesus makes us right with God, even though we are guilty of many sins.

Adam's sin led to condemnation.

But God's gift of grace leads to salvation and forgiveness of sin through Jesus Christ.

The sin of Adam caused death to rule over many.

But all who accept God's gift of righteousness through Jesus Christ will live in triumph over sin and death.

Adam's sin brought condemnation for everyone.

But Christ's death and resurrection brings a right relationship with God and new life for everyone who believes.

Because Adam disobeyed God, all people became sinners.

But because Jesus obeyed God, many sinners will have eternal life through Jesus Christ, our Lord.

ROMANS 6

Passage: "Don't you realize that you become the slave of whatever you choose to obey? You can be a slave to sin, which leads to death, or you can choose to obey God, which leads to righteous living."

Reflection:

Before knowing Jesus as your Lord and Savior, you let yourself be a slave to impurity, and you spiraled deeper and deeper into sin. As you did whatever you felt like doing—not caring about God or others—you became more enslaved to sin, and your life got increasingly worse. Now you are a slave to righteous living, which leads to holiness.

Before Jesus, you were a slave to sin and did shameful things that end in eternal doom. Now you are a slave of a loving God, free from the power of sin, and you do things that result in eternal life.

Since your old sinful self was crucified with Christ, consider yourself dead to the power of sin and alive to God through Jesus Christ. For the wages of sin is death, but the free gift of God is eternal life through Jesus Christ, our Lord.

ROMANS 7

Passage: "So we can see how terrible sin really is. It uses God's good commands for its own evil purposes."

Reflection:

Sin enslaves. Sin deceives. Sin takes what is of God—what is holy, right, and good—and twists it into something evil.

If we obey God's commands, given to us in the Bible, we will find life through them. But Satan is a destroyer of life, and he is the spirit behind all sin and wickedness. He is the one who makes people think that what is detestable to God is acceptable, what is evil to God is good, and what is wrong to God is right.

Who can free us from this life that is dominated by sin and death? The answer is Jesus Christ, our Lord. When we are united with the One who was raised from the dead, we are released from the power of sin and death. When Jesus is our Lord, we are no longer captive to the old way of living, but we are free to live in obedience to God by the power of the Holy Spirit. Thank God!

ROMANS 8

Passage: "The Spirit of God, who raised Jesus from the dead, lives in you. And just as God raised Christ Jesus from the dead, he will give life to your mortal bodies by the same Spirit living within you."

Reflection:

We who have the Spirit of Christ living in us belong to God. And because we belong to God, we are not dominated by the sinful nature, but we are led by the Spirit of God. When we surrender to the Holy Spirit and let him lead us and control how we think, the result is life and peace.

Since God himself chose us, called us, gave us right standing with himself through Jesus, and gives us his glory, we know that God will also cause everything to work together for our good. And although we must suffer on earth, just as Jesus suffered, it is nothing compared to the new bodies and future glory we look forward to sharing with God as his heirs.

Since God is for us, no one can ever be against us. No one dares to accuse us, and no one can condemn us. We belong to Jesus Christ, who gives us overwhelming victory, and nothing will ever be able to separate us from his love.

ROMANS 9

Passage: "Abraham, Isaac, and Jacob are their ancestors, and Christ himself was an Israelite as far as his human nature is concerned. And he is God, the one who rules over everything and is worthy of eternal praise! Amen."

Reflection:

Not everyone who is born into the nation of Israel is truly a member of God's family. God chooses people before they are even born, before they have done anything good or bad, to receive Christ and become members of his family. God chooses to show mercy and compassion to some, and he hardens the hearts of others. He selects some who will be spared from destruction and others he rejects. He calls those who were prepared in advance for glory to trust in Jesus, and others will stumble and fall over the great Rock in their path to heaven—Jesus the Messiah who is the only way—and they will never be saved.

If you are a child of the living God by placing your trust in Jesus Christ, thank your Creator for deciding to set you apart for himself and for showing you mercy—it's something you could neither choose nor work for. It's all of God who is worthy of eternal praise! Amen.

ROMANS 10

Passage: "Dear brothers and sisters, the longing of my heart and my prayer to God is for the people of Israel to be saved."

Reflection:

The people of Israel, despite their enthusiasm, have misdirected zeal for God and do not understand his way of making people right with himself. They think it's by obedience to all the commands that God gave Moses, but Jesus already accomplished the purpose for which the law was given. So it's by faith, believing in Jesus and calling on his name, that we are saved.

Even though salvation is offered to everyone, not everyone welcomes the Good News. But if you believe in your heart that God raised Jesus from the dead and openly declare your faith that Jesus is Lord, you will be saved. So don't be rebellious toward God's way of salvation, which you have been told about. Jesus has revealed himself to you with open arms, and anyone who trusts in him will never be disgraced.

ROMANS 11

Passage: "Oh, how great are God's riches and wisdom and knowledge! How impossible it is for us to understand his decisions and his ways!"

Reflection:

People are saved because of God's grace—his undeserved kindness in choosing them—not by their good works. And when God calls you and gives you the gift of salvation, it can never be withdrawn—no matter what.

Because the people of Israel were disobedient and turned down God's offer of salvation, he made salvation available to the rest of the world. We have received the blessing God promised to Abraham and his descendants because the people of Israel didn't believe in Christ.

May the people of Israel—and all people—turn from their unbelief, come to Christ, and be grafted into God's tree. May their hard hearts be softened to the Good News of salvation. And may they be set free from their rebellion and disobedience to share in God's grace and mercy and riches.

All glory to God forever! Amen.

ROMANS 12

Passage: "And so, dear brothers and sisters, I plead with you to give your bodies to God because of all he has done for you. Let them be a living and holy sacrifice—the kind he will find acceptable. This is truly the way to worship him."

Reflection:

To truly worship God, we must surrender our entire being to him—spirit, mind, and body. And as we read his Word daily and let him transform us into new people, here are several things we should not do:

Don't copy the behavior and customs of this world.

Don't think you are better than you really are.

Don't just pretend to love others—really love them.

Don't be too proud to enjoy the company of ordinary people.

Don't curse people who persecute you—pray for them.

Don't think you know it all.

Don't let evil conquer you—conquer evil by doing good.

ROMANS 13

Passage: "Love does no wrong to others, so love fulfills the requirements of God's law."

Reflection:

If you love your spouse, you will not be unfaithful in marriage. If you love your neighbor, you certainly won't want to murder them. If you love somebody, you will not steal from them. If you love others, you will not covet what belongs to them.

Since believers are clothed in the presence of the Lord Jesus Christ and belong to the day, we should remove dark deeds—wild parties, drunkenness, sexual promiscuity, immoral living, quarreling, jealousy—and get rid of them like dirty clothes. For when we do what is right and keep a clear conscience, not rebelling against what God has instituted, there is no need to live in fear of punishment.

ROMANS 14

Passage: "So why do you condemn another believer? Why do you look down on another believer?"

Reflection:

As brothers and sisters in Christ, we should not argue with each other about what we think is right or wrong— whether it's what we eat or drink, what day we worship God, what music we sing in church, or whatever we do. We belong to the Lord Jesus Christ and should live to honor him.

We will all stand before the judgment seat of God and give a personal account. So if someone believes something that God has permitted is wrong, then for that person, it is wrong. And if you do anything that you doubt is right or believe is wrong, you are sinning.

May we not cause one another to stumble or condemn someone for doing something they have decided is right. It's between them and God. Instead, let's aim for harmony in the church and try to build up the family of God.

ROMANS 15

Passage: "And the Scriptures give us hope and encouragement as we wait patiently for God's promises to be fulfilled."

Reflection:

As followers of Jesus, we are looking forward to the fulfillment of Scripture—the return of Christ, our new bodies, and our future home. But while we wait, we must learn to accept each other, help each other do what is right, and build each other up in the Lord. For it's when we live in harmony with one another that we can join together with one voice and give praise and glory to God.

While we wait for God's promises to be fulfilled, we must also learn to depend on Jesus and not ourselves. When we trust in ourselves, we are filled with stress and anxiety. But when we fully trust in Jesus, our source of hope, we are filled completely with joy and peace through the power of the Holy Spirit.

May our confidence be in Christ alone, and may God, who gives us hope, peace, and encouragement, be with us as we wait patiently for the Messiah's return. Amen.

ROMANS 16

Passage: "Watch out for people who cause divisions and upset people's faith by teaching things contrary to what you have been taught."

Reflection:

A smooth talker with glowing words that deceive people—this is a description of a person who is serving their own personal interests rather than serving the Lord. Stay away from these kinds of people. Instead, be wise in doing right by knowing what is right. This comes from reading the truth of the Bible. When you read God's Word, he will teach you what is right and give you the wisdom and strength to do it.

Someday soon, the God of peace will crush Satan under his feet, and we won't have to worry about deceivers. Until then, may the grace of our Lord Jesus be with you and help you stay innocent of any wrong.

✧ ✧ ✧

The Book of
1 CORINTHIANS

1 CORINTHIANS 1

Passage: "The message of the cross is foolish to those who are headed for destruction! But we who are being saved know it is the very power of God."

Reflection:

People can never know God through human wisdom or intelligence because God has made the wisdom of this world look foolish. God chose things the world considers foolish to shame those who think they are wise, things that are powerless to shame those who are powerful, and things that count as nothing to bring to nothing what the world considers important.

So-called brilliant philosophers and scholars say that the message of salvation through the crucifixion of Christ is foolish nonsense. But those who are called by God to salvation know that Christ is the very power and wisdom of God.

Christ makes us right with God.

Christ makes us pure and holy.

And Christ frees us from sin.

Reading:

1 CORINTHIANS 2

Passage: "But we understand these things, for we have the mind of Christ."

Reflection:

No one can know your thoughts except your own spirit, and no one can know God's thoughts except God's own Spirit. And since we have received God's Holy Spirit when we received Jesus as our Savior, we can know the wonderful things God gives us—from his Spirit to our spirit in open communication. We don't learn these things from reading books or going to school. We learn them directly from God.

People who do not have Christ do not have the Holy Spirit, and they can't receive truths from God. It all sounds foolish to them, and they can't understand. Only those who have received Jesus will be shown God's deep secrets by the Holy Spirit. Only those who have the Holy Spirit can understand God.

1 CORINTHIANS 3

Passage: "Everything belongs to you, and you belong
            to Christ, and Christ belongs to God."

Reflection:

Before we became a child of God through salvation, someone planted the seeds of the Good News in our hearts. Then, someone watered the seeds. But God made the seeds grow. And when it was time, we believed and received Jesus as our Savior and Lord.

Growing up to a mature Christian is a life-long process that requires the daily nourishment found in the Bible. As infants in Christ, we were fed Bible baby food, like milk, to help us grow stronger. As we continue to grow and eat the solid food of the Bible, our sinful nature becomes weaker, and our spirit becomes stronger. Being a spiritually healthy child of God is important because the Holy Spirit lives in us, and we are the holy temple of God. So we must prioritize taking good care of ourselves—spirit, mind, and body.

1 CORINTHIANS 4

Passage: "For the Kingdom of God is not just a lot of
talk; it is living by God's power."

Reflection:

As believers and faithful servants of Jesus Christ,
we must remember that everything we have has been
given to us as a gift from God. We must not become
arrogant people who make judgments about others—the
Lord will examine and judge everyone. Instead, we must
remain dedicated to Christ even though the world treats
us like garbage and sees us as fools.

May we, as beloved children of God, bless those who
curse us and be patient with those who abuse us. And
may our heavenly Father treat us with love and a gentle
spirit, giving each of us whatever praise is due.

1 CORINTHIANS 5

Passage: "I meant that you are not to associate with anyone who claims to be a believer yet indulges in sexual sin, or is greedy, or worships idols, or is abusive, or is a drunkard, or cheats people."

Reflection:

Sin starts out like a little yeast that quickly spreads through the whole batch of dough. So, as members of God's family, we are to avoid people inside the church who claim to be believers but are actively practicing a sinful way of life. Don't even eat with such people.

This does not mean that we are to avoid witnessing to unbelievers who are living in sin. We would have to leave the world and go to heaven to keep away from all wickedness and evil. According to Scriptures, it is not our responsibility to judge people outside the church, but it is our responsibility to judge and remove wicked people from inside the church who live immoral lifestyles of sin.

1 CORINTHIANS 6

Passage: "Don't you realize that your bodies are actually parts of Christ?"

Reflection:

Should a believer take their body, which is a part of Christ, and commit sexual sin? Never! Run from sexual sin—adultery, prostitution, and homosexuality to name a few—because no other sin affects your body like sexual sin does.

As followers of Jesus, we have been cleansed, made holy, and made right with God. When we called on the name of the Lord Jesus Christ, our body became the temple of the Holy Spirit who lives in us and was given to us by God. We do not belong to ourselves. God redeemed us with the high price of the precious blood of Christ. So fill your mind with the things of God and do not let sin control the way you live. Do not give in to sinful desires, but instead, honor God with your body.

1 CORINTHIANS 7

Passage: "For the world as we know it will soon pass
away."

Reflection:

The time that remains until Christ returns is very
short. So Christians should not be absorbed with their
possessions or attached to the things of the world. Don't
be enslaved by the world but be a slave of Christ. Spend
your time doing the Lord's work and thinking about
how to please him.

As far as being married or single, we should do
whatever will help us serve the Lord best, with as few
distractions as possible. It's good to stay single, but it's
better to marry than to burn with lust. Once a believer is
married, the Lord commands that a wife must not leave
her husband, and a husband must not leave his wife. If
their spouse dies, they are free to marry again, but only
to a person who loves the Lord.

1 CORINTHIANS 8

Passage: "There is one God, the Father, by whom all things were created, and for whom we live. And there is one Lord, Jesus Christ, through whom all things were created and through whom we live."

Reflection:

Some people think of idols as being real, but we know that an idol is not really a god and that there is only one God. Even so, some believers will not eat meat that has been offered to idols because it would violate their conscience. It's true that we can't win God's approval by what we eat or don't eat, but we must act in love toward other believers and not encourage them to do something they believe is wrong. If we cause another believer to stumble and sin, we are not only sinning against them, but we are sinning against Christ too.

1 CORINTHIANS 9

Passage: "Yes, I try to find common ground with everyone, doing everything I can to save some."

Reflection:

Paul was compelled by God to preach the Good News. It was his God-given assignment. So Paul, in order to bring many people to Christ, became like the people he was with. When he was with the Jews, he followed the Jewish law. When he was with the Gentiles, he did not follow the Jewish law. But he always obeyed the law of Christ.

As believers in Jesus Christ, we must also find common ground in order to relate to people. It's when we connect with others that it is easier to lead them into a saving relationship with Jesus.

May we lead a life with purpose in every step. May we share the Good News and enjoy the blessings of Jesus Christ. And may we look forward to the eternal prize that awaits us at the end of the race.

1 CORINTHIANS 10

Passage: "These things happened to them as examples for us. They were written down to warn us who live at the end of the age."

Reflection:

Most of the people of Israel, who were guided by God in a cloud and who drank from the spiritual rock (which was Christ), did not please God. They indulged in pagan revelry. They worshiped idols. They craved evil things. So God scattered their bodies in the wilderness. They engaged in sexual immortality, and 23,000 of them died in one day. They put the Lord to the test and died from snakebites. They grumbled at God and were destroyed by the angel of death.

Learn from the Israelites and do not rouse the Lord's jealousy. Don't mix Jesus and the world. It's like drinking from the cup of the Lord and the cup of demons, too. Whatever you do, do it ALL for the glory of God.

1 CORINTHIANS 11

Passage: On the night when he was betrayed, the Lord
Jesus took some bread and gave thanks to
God for it. Then he broke it in pieces and said,
"This is my body, which is given for you. Do
this to remember me."

Reflection:

The Lord's Supper, or communion, is taken by
believers in Jesus Christ to remember the sacrifice he
made for us on the cross—his broken body and shed
blood. Before taking communion, the Bible says that
we should examine ourselves to make sure we are in
a right relationship with God. If we are not, we are
sinning against the body and blood of Jesus by accepting
communion, and we are drinking God's judgment on
ourselves.

God's judgment of Christians is different than God's
judgment of non-Christians. Believers are judged with
divine discipline, which may sometimes be manifested
as weakness, sickness, or death. God's judgment reserved
for the unbelieving world is eternal condemnation in
the pit of destruction. But there is no condemnation for
those who belong to Jesus Christ.

1 CORINTHIANS 12

Passage: "All of you together are Christ's body, and each of you is a part of it."

Reflections:

Speaking to believers, Paul explained that each one of us is a part of the body of Christ, and God has put each part just where he wants it. Like the human body has many parts, so does the body of Christ. We all need each other to function properly, and we must all care for each other in order for there to be harmony. If one part of the body suffers, all the other parts suffer, too. If one part of the body is glad, so are the other parts.

Just as each part of the body functions differently, each person of the body of Christ is gifted with a special function. It is the same God who does the work in each of us, but in different ways. Some examples of spiritual gifts are wisdom, great faith, and special knowledge. But whatever spiritual gifts the Holy Spirit has decided to give you, he alone is the source of them all. May we be thankful for the spiritual gifts we have received and use them to help others and bring honor and great glory to our heavenly Father.

1 CORINTHIANS 13

Passage: "Three things will last forever—faith, hope, and love—and the greatest of these is love."

Reflection:

If we could do all things but didn't love others, we would be nothing.

- Love is patient and kind, not jealous, boastful, proud, or rude.
- Love never gives up—it endures through every circumstance.

If we understood all things and had faith that would move mountains but didn't love others, we would know nothing.

- Love doesn't demand its own way. It isn't irritable. It keeps no record of being wronged.
- Love never loses faith.

If we sacrificed everything—even our body—but didn't love others, we would have gained nothing.

- Love rejoices when the truth wins, not about injustice.
- Love is always hopeful.

So, no matter what I believe, say, or do, without love, I am nothing.

- Love will last forever!

1 CORINTHIANS 14

Passage: "If you speak to people in words they don't understand, how will they know what you are saying? You might as well be talking into empty space."

Reflection:

As followers of Jesus, the words we speak matter. Whether we are at church, home, work, or in the community, what we say should encourage people. Our words should strengthen those who are weak. Our voice should comfort those who need comfort. And our speech should help those who need help. We should use language that is understandable, especially when explaining spiritual things, so people can listen, learn, and respond as the Holy Spirit leads. But our highest goal should be that what we say and how we say it reflects the love of Jesus Christ.

1 CORINTHIANS 15

Passage: "I passed on to you what was most important and what has also been passed on to me. Christ died for our sins just as the Scriptures said. He was buried, and he was raised from the dead on the third day, just as the Scriptures said."

Reflection:

Why is it important that Jesus Christ was resurrected from the dead?

Because anyone who believes in Jesus and belongs to him by faith will also be raised from the dead. Our mortal bodies will be transformed into immortal bodies when the trumpet sounds. In the blink of an eye, all believers who have died will be raised to live forever, and all believers who are living at that time will be transformed instantly. Our weak and broken earthly bodies will become strong and glorious heavenly bodies.

Because Jesus was resurrected from the dead, death has lost its sting. Because Jesus was resurrected from the dead, death is swallowed up in victory. Thank God!

1 CORINTHIANS 16

Passage: "Be on guard. Stand firm in the faith. Be courageous. Be strong. And do everything with love."

Reflection:

Although many oppose the Lord's work, may we stand firm in the faith and walk through the doors that God opens. Although people may try to intimidate Christians, may we be courageous in our service to God's people. Although we are treated with contempt by others, may we be strong and serve God with devotion, giving our time, talent, and treasure to ministry. As brothers and sisters in Christ, may we gather together for church meetings and be on guard against attacks from the enemy, who does not love the Lord. May we hold tight to our convictions and do everything with love, encouraging each other to serve well. May the grace and blessings of the Lord Jesus be with us all.

✧ ✧ ✧

The Book of
2 CORINTHIANS

2 CORINTHIANS 1

Passage: "We were crushed and overwhelmed beyond our ability to endure, and we thought we would never live through it."

Reflection:

Have you ever heard someone say, "God won't give you more than you can handle?" That is not true. Just as God allowed Paul to be crushed and overwhelmed BEYOND HIS ABILITY, sometimes God will give us more than we can handle in our own strength. Why? So we will stop relying on ourselves and learn to rely on God.

Do you think that God, who raised Jesus from the dead, is incapable of taking care of you? Rather than striving to rescue yourself from the pressures and problems of life, decide to place your trust in Jesus (who always does what he says) and learn to rely on him. Over time and through experience, you will gain skill in reliance—that's what learning is.

Jesus did rescue you from sin and death. He will rescue you from today's troubles. And he will continue to rescue you forever. Amen!

2 CORINTHIANS 2

Passage: "Our lives are a Christ-like fragrance rising up to God."

Reflection:

After we invite Jesus into our hearts to be our Lord and Savior, God uses us to spread the knowledge of Christ everywhere. To people who are being saved by what we say, we are like sweet smelling, life-giving perfume. But to people who choose death and doom over Jesus, we are a dreadful smell.

In our own strength, we are not adequate to do anything. But our heavenly Father is always watching over us, and he will not let Satan outsmart us. God will overcome all obstacles and pave the way for us to confidently share the gospel and teach the Word. And we will soon discover that in Christ, God is leading us along in one perpetual victory parade!

2 CORINTHIANS 3

Passage: "And this veil can be removed only by believing in Christ."

Reflection:

Before a person believes in Christ, their heart is covered with a veil, so they can't see the light of the Good News or understand the message about Jesus, who is the exact likeness of God. Their mind is hardened by Satan, the god of this world, so they can't understand or believe the truth of the Bible.

After we believe in Christ, the Holy Spirit allows us to see spiritual truths. He transforms us to be more and more like Jesus. And he changes us so we can reflect the glory of the Lord.

When we turn to Jesus Christ as our Savior, we are made right with God. We are given spiritual life, spiritual minds, and spiritual eyes. The veil is taken away. Hallelujah!

2 CORINTHIANS 4

Passage: "So we don't look at the troubles we can see now; rather, we fix our gaze on things that cannot be seen. For the things we see now will soon be gone, but the things we cannot see will last forever."

Reflection:

Our bodies are like fragile clay jars with a great treasure inside—the light of Jesus. When we suffer, our bodies share in the physical death of Jesus, but the spiritual life of Jesus is also seen in our bodies. How? Even though we are pressed by troubles and get knocked down, we are not driven to despair, we are not destroyed, and we never give up. Because the great power inside our fragile bodies that gives us strength to endure is not from ourselves—it is from Almighty God.

Though our temporary bodies are dying, our eternal spirits are being renewed and strengthened every day. The physical troubles we experience in this life will produce a spiritual glory that lasts forever when God raises us and presents us to himself. Since our bodies will soon be gone, but our spirits will last forever, we shouldn't focus on the physical, but instead, we should fix our eyes on the eternal.

2 CORINTHIANS 5

Passage: "This means that anyone who belongs to Christ has become a new person. The old life is gone; a new life has begun!"

Reflection:

God made Christ, who was born of a virgin and who never sinned, to be the offering for our sin. By believing in Jesus' death, burial, and resurrection, and by accepting God's gift of salvation, our sins are not counted against us. Through Christ, we are made right with God. We have a new life, and we become ambassadors for Christ to reconcile others to God.

Jesus Christ died for everyone, and we who receive him as our Savior and Lord will live for him and not ourselves because we have died to our old life. While we live here on earth, our goal is to please Jesus and let his love control us. Then, one day, we will put on our heavenly bodies like new clothing and be at home with the Lord. Until then, we live by believing and not by seeing. We live by faith in Jesus.

2 CORINTHIANS 6

Passage: "Indeed, the 'right time' is now. Today is the day of salvation."

Reflection:

When you accept God's marvelous gift of salvation, don't stop there. Live in such a way that no one will stumble into sin because of you, and no one will find fault with you. Patiently endure troubles and hardships. Prove yourself by showing sincere love and kindness. Serve God whether you are honored or slandered by people. And give spiritual riches to others.

Whether materially wealthy or poor, in Christ, we have everything. The Lord Almighty is our Father, our Savior, and our Friend—and we are his sons and daughters. We are the temple of the Living God. Therefore, don't team up with unbelievers. How can light live with darkness? Come out from among them. How can righteousness partner with wickedness? Separate yourselves from them. How can there be harmony between Christ and the devil?

2 CORINTHIANS 7

Passage: "Because we have these promises, dear friends, let us cleanse ourselves from everything that can defile our body or spirit. And let us work toward complete holiness because we fear God."

Reflection:

It can be painful to hear the truth of the Bible, especially when we are convicted by the Holy Spirit of sin in our lives. But when the pain causes you to repent to God and change your ways, it is the kind of sorrow that God wants you to have—godly sorrow.

Godly sorrow produces earnestness, zeal, and a desire to do everything necessary to make things right. Godly sorrow leads us away from sin and results in salvation. But worldly sorrow lacks repentance and results in spiritual death.

2 CORINTHIANS 8

Passage: "You know the generous grace of our Lord Jesus Christ. Though he was rich, yet for your sakes, he became poor, so that by his poverty, he could make you rich."

Reflection:

The first act of giving that God wants is for a person to give themselves to the Lord Jesus Christ through salvation. After that, give in proportion to what you have. Whatever you give is acceptable if you give it eagerly. And give according to what you have, not what you don't have.

The ministry of giving includes giving of your time, talents, and treasure. When we give of our time and talent, showing an eagerness to help, it glorifies the Lord. And when we have plenty and enthusiastically give to those in need, it makes life easier for them and brings honor to God.

2 CORINTHIANS 9

Passage: "Remember this—a farmer who plants only a few seeds will get a small crop. But the one who plants generously will get a generous crop."

Reflection:

Everything comes from God. He is the one who provides the seed for the farmer and then bread to eat. He is the one who provides income and then produces a harvest of generosity in Christians. As a result, the needs of others are met, believers and non-believers, and glory is given to God.

When we share freely and give cheerfully, God will generously provide for all our needs. Yes, he will enrich us in every way, and we will have plenty left over to share with others. May we joyfully thank God for his grace and gifts, which are too wonderful for words!

2 CORINTHIANS 10

Passage: "We are human, but we don't wage war as humans do."

Reflection:

As followers of Jesus Christ, we know that pride is an obstacle that keeps people from knowing God. So, rebellious thoughts must be captured, false arguments must be destroyed, and the walls of human reasoning must be knocked down using the mighty weapons of God.

When people compare themselves with each other, using themselves rather than Christ as the standard, they are showing their ignorance. And when people commend themselves, it doesn't count for much. The important thing is for the Lord to commend them. So if you want to boast, boast only about the Lord. And if you want praise, seek it from God, not people.

2 CORINTHIANS 11

Passage: "But I fear that somehow your pure and undivided devotion to Christ will be corrupted, just as Eve was deceived by the cunning ways of the serpent."

Reflection:

Don't be surprised when people preach a different Jesus, a different kind of spirit other than the Holy Spirit, or a different kind of gospel than is found in the Bible. But don't put up with it, and don't believe whatever anyone tells you. Compare what you hear to the truth of the Bible.

Even Satan, the father of lies, disguises himself as an angel of light. So it is no wonder that people who are not true believers in Jesus disguise themselves as Christians and deceive many people. These wicked people of darkness will enslave you. They are out to take everything you have and take advantage of you. They are not servants of righteousness, and in the end, they will get the punishment their evil deeds deserve.

2 CORINTHIANS 12

Passage: "For when I am weak, then I am strong."

Reflection:

The apostle Paul received wonderful revelations from God. But he also received a messenger from Satan to torment him in the flesh and to keep him from becoming proud and boastful. He doesn't tell us what it was, just that he wanted it gone. In fact, he asked the Lord three different times to take it away. But each time, Jesus said, "My grace is all you need. My power works best in weakness."

Beloved child of God, are you feeling weak from your hardships and troubles? Then, like Paul, you should be glad and even take pleasure in your weaknesses. Because it is when you are weak that the power of Christ can work through you. For when you are weak, then you are strong.

2 CORINTHIANS 13

Passage: "Be joyful. Grow to maturity. Encourage each other. Live in harmony and peace. Then the God of love and peace will be with you."

Reflection:

Test yourself. Examine yourself to see if your faith is genuine. If you know that Jesus Christ is in you and among you, then you have passed the test.

Do the right thing. Do not do what is wrong by refusing correction. Listen to God and obey his Word, and then you will be strengthened.

Stand for the truth. Do not oppose the truth. The Bible is truth.

May the grace of the Lord Jesus Christ, the love of God, and the fellowship of the Holy Spirit be with you.

✧ ✧ ✧

The Book of
GALATIANS

GALATIANS 1

Passage: "Jesus gave his life for our sins, just as God our Father planned, in order to rescue us from this evil world in which we live."

Reflection:

This is the Good News! So don't be fooled by people who twist the truth about Jesus Christ and pretend to teach another way of salvation. Jesus is the only way. And those who teach any other way will be cursed.

Before we were ever born, God chose us, by his grace, to be rescued so that we would belong to him forever. And when we came to Christ, we were changed by the power of the Holy Spirit into different people. The apostle Paul went from violently persecuting God's church to preaching the very faith he tried to destroy. Therefore, brothers and sisters in Christ, people pleasing is not our goal. We are servants of Christ. So do not worry about winning the approval of people, but of God.

GALATIANS 2

Passage: "My old self has been crucified with Christ. It is no longer I who live, but Christ lives in me. So I live in this earthly body by trusting in the Son of God, who loved me and gave himself for me."

Reflection:

A person is made right with God by faith in Jesus Christ, not by obeying the law or by following manmade rules, rituals, and regulations. So when we believe in Jesus Christ, who gave himself for us, we are made right with God. No one will ever be made right with God by following religious laws and traditions. If that were true, then there was no need for Christ to die for us.

Legalistic people will try to enslave you by forcing you to follow their religious regulations and preferences. But we don't live by following the rule of law. We live by trusting in the Son of God. So don't let others take away the freedom you have in Jesus Christ.

GALATIANS 3

Passage: "Let me ask you one question: Did you receive
the Holy Spirit by obeying the law of Moses?
Of course not! You received the Spirit because
you believed the message you heard about
Christ."

Reflection:

The law of Moses was given to show people their
sins. It was designed to last only until the coming of the
Messiah, Jesus Christ. So the law was the guardian of
the people until Christ came. It protected them until
they could be made right with God by faith. So now
that Jesus Christ and the way of faith has come, people
no longer need the law as their guardian.

It is through faith in Jesus that a person has eternal
life. It is through faith in Christ that a person becomes
a child of God. And we who belong to Christ are the
true children of Abraham, his heirs, and God's promise
to Abraham belongs to us.

GALATIANS 4

Passage: "So, dear brothers and sisters, we are not children of the slave woman; we are children of the free woman."

Reflection:

Abraham had two sons. Ishmael was born from Hagar, the slave wife of Abraham. He was born as a result of a human attempt to fulfill God's promise. Hagar represents God's first covenant, the law that enslaved people.

Isaac was born to Sarah, the freeborn wife of Abraham, when she was about 90 years old. Isaac was born as a result of God's own divine fulfillment of his promise. Sarah represents the heavenly Jerusalem.

God told Abraham to get rid of the slave and her son (first covenant, law) because the son of the slave woman will not share the inheritance with the free woman's son. Then, at just the right time, God sent his Son to replace the first covenant and buy freedom for us who were slaves to the law so that he could adopt us as his very own children. So now, only those who are God's children through Christ are his heirs. And only those who are born again by the divine power of the Holy Spirit (not a human attempt, works) will inherit the heavenly Jerusalem.

GALATIANS 5

Passage: "When you follow the desires of your sinful nature, the results are very clear: sexual immorality, impurity, lustful pleasures, idolatry, sorcery, hostility, quarreling, jealousy, outbursts of anger, selfish ambition, dissension, division, envy, drunkenness, wild parties, and other sins like these. Let me tell you again, as I have before, that anyone living that sort of life will not inherit the Kingdom of God."

Reflection:

The sinful nature desires to do evil and produces rotten fruit. But when you belong to Jesus and are directed by the Holy Spirit, the desires of your sinful nature are nailed to the cross and crucified.

If you let the Spirit guide you, then you won't do what your sinful nature craves. When you are living by the Spirit, you will produce the good fruit of love, joy, peace, patience, kindness, goodness, faithfulness, gentleness, and self-control. And as you follow the Spirit's leading in every part of your life, your faith will express itself in love.

GALATIANS 6

Passage: "Don't be misled—you cannot mock the justice of God. You will always harvest what you plant."

Reflection:

You harvest what you plant.

If you live to please your sinful nature, you will harvest decay and death. But if you live to please the Holy Spirit, you will harvest everlasting life.

Share each other's burdens.

Help people, especially your brothers and sisters in Christ, to get on and stay on the right path.

Pay attention to your own work.

Find satisfaction in a job well done. Don't compare yourself to anyone else. We are each responsible for our own conduct.

Do good to everyone.

Whenever you have the opportunity, you should do good to everyone, especially those in the family of faith.

Don't boast.

Never boast about anything—except the cross of Christ. What really matters is whether you have been transformed into a new creation, not the world's interest in you.

Never give up.

Don't get tired of doing what is good. At just the right time, you will reap a harvest of blessings!

✦ ✧ ✦

The Book of
EPHESIANS

EPHESIANS 1

Passage: "He is so rich in kindness and grace that he purchased our freedom with the blood of his Son and forgave our sins."

Reflection:

All praise to God the Father of our Lord Jesus Christ who:

Blessed us
with every spiritual blessing.

Loved us
even before he made the world.

Chose us
in advance to be holy and without fault in his eyes.

Adopts us
into his own family.

Brings us
to himself through Jesus Christ.

Poured out his grace on us
who belong to his Son.

Showered his kindness on us
along with wisdom and understanding.

Revealed to us
his plan to bring everything in heaven and earth
under the authority of Christ.

Unites us
with Christ.

Saves us
when we believe in Christ.

Identifies us
as his own.

Gives us
his Holy Spirit as his guarantee that we are his and
we will receive our promised inheritance.

All praise to God the Father of our Lord Jesus Christ!

EPHESIANS 2

Passage: "Once you were dead because of your disobedience and your many sins. You used to live in sin, just like the rest of the world, obeying the devil—the commander of the powers in the unseen world. He is the spirit at work in the hearts of those who refuse to obey God."

Reflection:

We are all born spiritually dead because of our sinful nature—without God and without hope. But God loves us so much that he saves us by his grace when we believe in Jesus Christ.

Salvation is a gift from God; it's not a reward for doing good things. When we ask Jesus to become our Lord and Savior, we are instantly born again and become spiritually alive. We become members of God's family, and along with other believers, we are joined together as a holy temple where God lives by his Spirit. Because we are united with Christ, who was raised from the dead, we will also be raised from the dead. And because of God's incredible grace and kindness toward us, we can look forward to the day when we will live with him in heaven for eternity!

EPHESIANS 3

Passage: "And may you have the power to understand, as all God's people should, how wide, how long, how high, and how deep his love is."

Reflection:

Everyone who believes the Good News shares equally in the riches inherited by God's children. We are all part of the same body of Christ. We all enjoy the promise of blessings and endless treasures because we belong to Jesus Christ. And we can all come boldly and confidently into God's presence through prayer because of Christ and our faith in him.

As we trust in Jesus, he will make his home in our hearts and empower us with inner strength through his Holy Spirit. As we experience the love of Christ, our lives are made complete and full. And as our roots grow deeper in the love of God, he will accomplish infinitely more than we ask or imagine through his mighty power at work within us.

All glory to God, the Creator of everything in heaven and on earth, forever and ever! Amen.

EPHESIANS 4

Passage: "Get rid of all bitterness, rage, anger, harsh words, and slander, as well as all types of evil behavior. Instead, be kind to each other, tender-hearted, forgiving one another, just as God through Christ Jesus has forgiven you."

Reflection:

Because God has identified believers in Jesus Christ as his own, we should not bring sorrow to his Holy Spirit by the way we live. Foul or abusive language does not fit who we are in Christ. Our words should be good, helpful, and encouraging to people who hear them. We should speak the truth in love.

Anger gives the devil a hold in our lives. So we must not let anger control us, and we should not let the sun go down with anger in our hearts. We, as Christians, are to forgive others, giving up our right to anger, whether we feel it's justified or not. We don't forgive others because they deserve it. We forgive them as an act of worship to God because you and I didn't deserve forgiveness either.

As we allow the Holy Spirit to renew our thoughts and attitudes, may our words and actions be righteous and holy. May we be humble, gentle, and patient with people, making allowances for each other's faults because of our love. And may we lead a life that is worthy of our calling and grow in every way more and more like Christ.

EPHESIANS 5

Passage: "Live a life filled with love, following the
example of Christ. He loved us and offered
himself as a sacrifice for us, a pleasing aroma
to God."

Reflection:

As followers of Jesus Christ, who has given you
light, live as people of the light. Carefully determine
what pleases the Lord and do it. Don't let there be any
immorality or impurity in your life. And don't live like
fools who participate in worthless deeds of darkness. As
God's people, let your life be filled with what is good
and right and true. Give thanks to God for everything
and be filled with the Holy Spirit.

Just as a man and woman are united in marriage,
so it is with Christ and the church. And just as Christ
cares for his body, the church, we must also care for and
submit to each other out of reverence for Christ.

Therefore, may we follow the example of Christ who
submitted to God. May we be holy and clean, washed
by the cleansing of God's Word. And may we live in the
light and imitate God in everything we do because we
are his dear children.

EPHESIANS 6

Passage: "A final word: Be strong in the Lord and in his mighty power. Put on all of God's armor so that you will be able to stand firm against all strategies of the devil."

Reflection:

Christians are in a battle every day. We are not fighting against flesh-and-blood enemies but against evil spirits of the dark, unseen world. So, each day, we must put on every piece of God's armor to be victorious in spiritual warfare.

The belt of truth will help you stand your ground against lies and deception. The body armor of God's righteousness will protect your heart and emotions against spiritual attacks. For shoes, put on the peace that comes from the Good News. The shield of faith will stop the fiery arrows of the devil. The helmet of salvation will protect your mind. And for offense, take the sword of the Spirit, which is the Word of God.

In addition to the armor of God, it is important to be persistent in our prayers for all believers everywhere so that we will all be able to resist the strategies of the devil and stand firm in this time of evil.

✧ ✧ ✧

The Book of
PHILIPPIANS

PHILIPPIANS 1

Passage: "Above all, you must live as citizens of heaven, conducting yourselves in a manner worthy of the Good News about Christ."

Reflection:

Brothers and sisters in Christ,

As citizens of heaven, we must understand what really matters—living pure and blameless lives until the day of Christ's return. I pray that we will be bold for Christ, not ashamed. I also pray that we will keep on growing in knowledge and understanding and that our love for God and others will overflow. Since we have been given the privilege of trusting in Christ, may our lives bring honor to Jesus as we confidently spread and fearlessly defend the Good News. May we stand and fight together for the faith and not be intimidated by the enemy, for they will be destroyed by God. And may the fruit of our salvation—our righteous character—bring much glory and praise to God.

May God our Father and the Lord Jesus Christ give you grace and peace.

PHILIPPIANS 2

Passage: "You must have the same attitude that Christ Jesus had."

Reflection:

The Lord Jesus Christ gave up his divine privileges as God the Son to be born as a human being. He lived his life on earth in humble obedience to God the Father, then he died on a cross like a criminal to pay for our sins. So, God elevated Jesus to the place of highest honor and gave him the name above all other names. And one day, at the name of Jesus Christ, every knee everywhere will bow and declare that Jesus is Lord to the glory of God the Father!

May our attitude be one of selflessness, servanthood, and sacrifice that puts the needs of others before ourselves.

PHILIPPIANS 3

Passage: "Yes, everything else is worthless when compared with the infinite value of knowing Christ Jesus, my Lord."

Reflection:

Human effort and strict obedience to religious laws are worthless because of what Jesus Christ has done for us. We can't work to earn our salvation. God's way of righteousness comes only through faith in Christ.

As followers of Jesus, we should pattern our lives after his, forget the past, and eagerly look forward to what lies ahead—the return of Christ. Because when Jesus returns as our Savior, he will change our weak mortal bodies into glorious bodies like his, and he will bring everything under his control. So let's rejoice as citizens of heaven, press on to the end of the race, and receive our heavenly prize!

PHILIPPIANS 4

Passage: "Fix your thoughts on what is true and honorable, and right, and pure, and lovely, and admirable. Think about things that are excellent and worthy of praise."

Reflection:

Don't worry about anything. Instead, pray about everything and give thanks to God for all he has done. Then, you will experience God's peace, which is far beyond our understanding.

Be content with whatever you have been given by God, whether it's a little or a lot. And be certain that if your name is written in the Book of Life, God will supply all your needs from his glorious riches.

Remember, no matter what difficult situation you are facing, you can do everything through Christ who gives you strength.

And as you live in Christ Jesus, may the peace of God guard your heart and mind, and may the God of peace be with you.

✧ ✧ ✧

The Book of
COLOSSIANS

COLOSSIANS 1

Passage: "Christ is the visible image of the invisible God. He existed before anything was created and is supreme over all creation, for through him, God created everything in the heavenly realms and on earth."

Reflection:

Jesus made the things we can see and the things we can't see. Everything was created through Jesus and for Jesus. Jesus existed before anything else. And Jesus holds all creation together. Jesus is the head of the church, which is his body. Jesus is the supreme beginning of all who rise from the dead. Jesus is first in everything.

Through Jesus, God reconciled everything to himself. And by the blood of Jesus on the cross, God reconciled sinners to himself. As believers, Jesus rescued us from the kingdom of darkness and transferred us to the Kingdom of Heaven. And because Jesus purchased our freedom and forgave our sins, we who were once God's enemies are now at peace with God.

Thank you, Jesus!

COLOSSIANS 2

Passage: "You were dead because of your sins and because your sinful nature was not yet cut away. Then God made you alive with Christ, for he forgave all our sins."

Reflection:

As a believer in Jesus Christ, you are complete through your union with him. You have died with Christ. You were buried with Christ, and you have been raised to new life by the mighty power of God.

When you received Jesus as your Savior, God canceled the record of the charges of sin against you and took it away by nailing it to the cross. When you came to Christ, he performed a spiritual circumcision—the cutting away of your sinful nature. Then, when you were baptized, you were buried with Christ and raised to new life.

Since Jesus is your Lord, follow him and let your roots grow down into him. Build your life on him, then your faith will grow strong, and you will overflow with thankfulness.

COLOSSIANS 3

Passage: "So let's strip off our old sinful nature and all its wicked deeds and put on our new nature."

Reflection:

Tender-hearted mercy, kindness, humility, gentleness, patience, and thankfulness. This is the clothing that we who are called and loved by God must wear. In addition, we must put on forgiveness, making allowances for each other's faults, and excusing anyone who offends us. And since Christ is our life, above all, we must clothe ourselves with love.

Whether at home or work or wherever we go, may we always remember that the Master we are serving is Christ. May we, who have died to this life and have been raised to new life with Christ, set our sights on the realities of heaven and think about the things of heaven, not the things of earth. And as we learn to know our Creator and become more like him, may we be good representatives of the Lord Jesus Christ in our character, conduct, and conversations.

COLOSSIANS 4

Passage: "Devote yourselves to prayer with an alert
mind and a thankful heart."

Reflection:

Pray that God will give you many opportunities to
clearly proclaim the message about Christ. Live wisely
among unbelievers. Let your conversation be full of grace.
And may God make you strong and fully confident that
you are following his will and carrying out the ministry
the Lord Jesus gave you.

✧ ✧ ✧

The Book of
1 THESSALONIANS

1 THESSALONIANS 1

Passage: "And they speak of how you are looking forward to the coming of God's Son from heaven—Jesus, whom God raised from the dead. He is the one who rescued us from the terrors of the coming judgment."

Reflection:

As believers, people who have received the Good News about Jesus with joy, we know that God loves us and has chosen us to be his own people. But how do we live a life of faith? We can learn much from the example of our brothers and sisters at the church in Thessalonica.

Despite the severe suffering it brought them, the church at Thessalonica turned from idols to serve the living and true God. Their lives were characterized by faithful work, loving deeds, and enduring hope. And the Word of the Lord rang out from them to people everywhere. May our faith in Jesus result in fruitful living that pleases God and gives people something wonderful to talk about!

1 THESSALONIANS 2

Passage: "For we speak as messengers approved by God to be entrusted with the Good News. Our purpose is to please God, not people. He alone examines the motives of our hearts."

Reflection:

Persecution from your own countrymen is not new to Christianity. The Jews persecuted their own people and prophets for believing in Jesus Christ—some even killed the Lord Jesus. People try to prevent the preaching of the Good News of salvation, but what they are really doing is piling up their own sins. Eventually, the anger of God will catch up with them.

Today, over 350 million Christians worldwide suffer persecution. Believers are being insulted, isolated, humiliated, discriminated, arrested, beaten, tortured, burned, or even killed for their faith. And as the return of the Lord Jesus gets closer, Satan is working overtime to bring about more extreme violence toward Christians. This life will not be lived without trouble, but God has called believers to share in his eternal Kingdom and glory, and one day, we will receive a reward and a crown for living in a way that God considers worthy.

1 THESSALONIANS 3

Passage: "Night and day we pray earnestly for you, asking God to let us see you again to fill the gaps in your faith."

Reflection:

Christians need other Christians. Just as Timothy went to see the believers at Thessalonica, we should spend time with other believers so that we can strengthen, encourage, and pray for one another, especially in times of trouble. It helps our brothers and sisters in Christ who are suffering to see us remain strong in our faith and stand firm in the Lord, especially during difficult times.

When we sacrifice our time to gather with other believers, it is an act of love for God and his holy people. I pray that the Lord Jesus will make our hearts strong and our love for God and all people grow and overflow. Amen.

1 THESSALONIANS 4

Passage: "And now, dear brothers and sisters, we want you to know what will happen to the believers who have died so you will not grieve like people who have no hope."

Reflection:

When the Lord Jesus comes down from heaven, we will hear a commanding shout, the voice of an archangel, and a trumpet call of God. Then, the believers who have died will rise up from their graves into the clouds. Next, the believers who are still alive on earth will be lifted up into the clouds to meet the Lord Jesus in the air. Then we will all be with the Lord forever!

While we wait for Jesus to come and get us, Christians are urged to live in a way that pleases God. So stay away from sexual sin. Love one another. Mind your own business. And live quiet lives in holiness and honor.

1 THESSALONIANS 5

Passage: "But you aren't in the dark about these things, dear brothers and sisters, and you won't be surprised when the day of the Lord comes like a thief. For you are all children of the light and of the day; we don't belong to darkness and night. So be on your guard, not asleep like the others. Stay alert and be clearheaded."

Reflection:

The return of the Lord Jesus will come suddenly and unexpectedly. So those who belong to him—and will not experience his anger—must always be ready and live each day as children of the light:

Live peacefully with each other.

Warn those who are lazy.

Encourage those who are timid.

Take care of those who are weak.

Love and appreciate your spiritual leaders.

Be patient with everyone.

Do good to all people.

Always be joyful.

Never stop praying.

Be thankful in all circumstances.

Do not suppress the Holy Spirit.

Stay away from every kind of evil.

Now, may God keep you completely blameless until the day when our Lord Jesus Christ comes again. And may the amazing grace and peace of God be with you always.

✧ ✧ ✧

The Book of
2 THESSALONIANS

2 THESSALONIANS 1

Passage: "And in his justice, he will pay back those who persecute you."

Reflection:

When Christians experience hardships, we are to remain faithful to Jesus and endure by the power of his grace. In the midst of persecution, we must focus on Jesus and on living a life worthy of God's call. Then, despite our suffering, the Lord will enable us to accomplish all the good things he has planned for us to do.

When Jesus appears from heaven with his mighty angels, he will bring judgment on those who persecute Christians and refuse to know him as their Lord and Savior. They will be punished forever in flaming fire—eternally destroyed and separated from God. But all who believe will have rest on that day when Jesus our Savior returns. And we, God's holy people, will give praise, honor, and glory to the Lord for his love, faithfulness, and justice.

2 THESSALONIANS 2

Passage: "This man will come to do the work of Satan with counterfeit power and signs and miracles."

Reflection:

Prior to the second coming of the Lord Jesus Christ, there will be a great rebellion against God, and the man of sin, lawlessness, and destruction will be revealed. He will exalt himself, sit in the temple of God, and claim that he himself is God.

This man, known as the antichrist, will come to do the work of Satan after Jesus suddenly removes all Christians from earth and takes them to heaven. Then all hell will break loose on earth!

The antichrist will use every kind of evil deception to fool the people who were left behind by Jesus—people on their way to destruction because they refuse to accept the truth about Christ. So they will believe the lies, signs, and miracles of the antichrist, and they will be condemned for enjoying evil rather than believing the truth.

The time for the antichrist to be revealed has not yet come. However, the spirit of the antichrist is already at work in the world. But when the day of the Lord does come and Jesus returns to earth, he will blow away the antichrist with the breath of his mouth and destroy him by the splendor of his coming! Hallelujah!

2 THESSALONIANS 3

Passage: "And now, dear brothers and sisters, we give you this command in the name of our Lord Jesus Christ: Stay away from all believers who live idle lives and don't follow the tradition they received from us."

Reflection:

Followers of Jesus should not live idle lives or refuse to work—and we should stay away from believers who do. We should be busy working to earn a living, serving God, and doing good. Then we won't have time to meddle in other people's business.

Pray that the Lord's message will spread rapidly and be received wherever it goes. Pray that believers will be rescued from evil. And pray that the Lord will help you to fully understand and express the love of God. May the Lord of peace himself give you patient endurance in every situation and peace at all times.

✧ ✧ ✧

The Book of
1 TIMOTHY

1 TIMOTHY 1

Passage: "In my insolence, I persecuted his people. But
God had mercy on me because I did it in
ignorance and unbelief. Oh, how generous
and gracious our Lord was! He filled me with
the faith and love that come from Christ
Jesus."

Reflection:

The apostle Paul, prior to coming to faith in Jesus,
used to blaspheme the name of Christ and persecute his
people. But God used him as an example so that even
the worst sinners would realize that they too can believe
in Jesus and receive eternal life.

Jesus Christ came into the world to save sinners, which
includes you and me. We were all lawless, rebellious,
ungodly, and sinful people. But God had mercy on us
when we accepted Jesus as our Savior, and now he has
appointed us to serve him. So, as God's beloved children,
we should be filled with love that comes from a pure
heart, a clear conscience, and genuine faith so that we
can help others live lives of faith in God.

1 TIMOTHY 2

Passage: "There is one God and one Mediator who can reconcile God and humanity—the man Christ Jesus. He gave his life to purchase freedom for everyone."

Reflection:

God wants everyone to be saved and to understand the truth—only through Jesus can people be reconciled to God. Only through Jesus can we have freedom from sin and death.

As Christians, we are to pray for all people, asking God to help them. We are to intercede on their behalf and give thanks for them. It also pleases God when we intercede in prayer for leaders and people who are in authority so that we can live quiet, dignified lives.

May we pray to God with holy hands and hearts that are free from anger, disputing, and quarreling. May we be attractive by the good things we do. And may we live our lives in faith, love, holiness, and modesty.

1 TIMOTHY 3

Passage: "I am writing these things to you now, even
though I hope to be with you soon, so that if
I am delayed, you will know how people must
conduct themselves in the household of God."

Reflection:

Above reproach. Faithful. Self-control. Live wisely.
Clear conscience. Good reputation. Integrity. Gentle.
Not love money. Enjoy having guests. Committed to
the faith.

Although most Christians will not be leaders in the
church, we are members of the household of God. So,
we would do well to aspire to have the character that
the Bible describes for people in the honorable positions
of elders and deacons. Then, we will be rewarded
with respect from others, and we will have increased
confidence in our faith in Jesus Christ.

1 TIMOTHY 4

Passage: "Physical training is good, but training for godliness is much better, promising benefits in this life and in the life to come."

Reflection:

In these last times, some people are turning away from the true faith to follow deceptive spirits and teachings that come from demons. So focus on reading the truth of the Bible, keep a close watch on how you live, and stay true to what is right. Remember, our hope is in the living God who is the Savior of all people—that is why we strive to work hard.

For your own good and the salvation of those who observe you, be an example in what you say, in the way you live, in your love, and in your purity. And may you experience an increase in unshakable faith in response to God's faithfulness.

1 TIMOTHY 5

Passage: "The good deeds of some people are obvious.
And the good deeds done in secret will
someday come to light."

Reflection:

God sees our sins and our good deeds—those that
are obvious and those that are done in secret. So keep
yourself pure, don't be led astray, and don't share in the
sins of others. Treat people with respect, as if they are
members of your family. And never speak harshly to an
older person.

For the people who are members of our family, let's
please God and show godliness at home by taking care
of our relatives—those in our own home and parents
or grandparents who have no one else to care for them.
They are our first responsibility. And believers who won't
care for their relatives are worse than unbelievers.

1 TIMOTHY 6

Passage: "For the love of money is the root of all kinds of evil."

Reflection:

People who long to be rich often fall into temptation and are trapped by foolish and harmful desires that plunge them into ruin and destruction. Their craving for money causes them to wander away from God and the true faith, and eventually, they are pierced with many sorrows.

People who are wealthy in this world should not become proud or trust in their money, which is so unreliable. Instead, their trust should be in God, who richly gives us all we need for our enjoyment. May we be rich in good works and use our money to do good and help others, then we will be building a foundation for the future and storing up treasure in heaven!

✧ ✧ ✧

The Book of
2 TIMOTHY

2 TIMOTHY 1

Passage: "For God has not given us a spirit of fear and timidity, but of power, love, and self-discipline."

Reflection:

Never be ashamed to tell people about the Lord Jesus Christ, and if necessary, be ready to suffer for the Good News. For God showed us his grace through Jesus Christ and called us to live a holy life. He broke the power of death and illuminated the way to life and immortality through the Good News.

May we, those who are saved and called by God (not because we deserved it), live through the power of the Holy Spirit within us. May we serve God with a clear conscience, hold on to the wholesome teachings we have learned, and guard the precious truth of the Holy Bible. And may God show us special kindness and give us strength to live by faith and love.

2 TIMOTHY 2

Passage: "Always remember that Jesus Christ, a descendant of King David, was raised from the dead. This is the Good News I preach. And because I preach this Good News, I am suffering and have been chained like a criminal. But the word of God cannot be chained."

Reflection:

Good soldiers of Jesus Christ must endure suffering, especially when it may bring salvation and eternal life to those God has chosen. Also, soldiers don't get tied up in the matters of civilian life. So focus on pleasing the Lord Jesus, not the world. Turn away from evil and avoid worthless, foolish talk that leads to godless behavior and spreads like cancer.

Again, keep yourself pure and ready for the Master to use you for all kinds of good work. Pursue righteous living, faithfulness, love, and peace. Don't quarrel. Be kind to everyone. Gently instruct people who are held captive by the devil and oppose the truth. Maybe God will change their hearts, and they will come to their senses, escaping the devil's trap.

2 TIMOTHY 3

Passage: "All Scripture is inspired by God and is useful to teach us what is true and to make us realize what is wrong in our lives. It corrects us when we are wrong and teaches us to do what is right."

Reflection:

Love only themselves and their money. Boastful. Proud. Scoffing at God. Disobedient. Ungrateful. Consider nothing sacred. Unloving. Unforgiving. Slander others. No self-control. Cruel. Hate what is good. Betray their friends. Love pleasure rather than God. Depraved minds. Counterfeit faith. Act religious but reject Jesus.

This is how the Bible—the inspired Word of God—describes people living in the last days. And that's why it is more important than ever to study Scripture every day. It gives us wisdom to receive the salvation that comes only by trusting in Jesus Christ and teaches us how to live a godly life in these very difficult last days.

2 TIMOTHY 4

Passage: "For a time is coming when people will no longer listen to sound and wholesome teaching."

Reflection:

As followers of Jesus, we must be prepared to proclaim the Word of God whether or not the time is favorable. Today, people often don't want to hear the truth of the Bible. They follow their own desires instead of God and want to hear only what makes them feel good. But we must patiently correct them, work at telling them the Good News, and not be afraid of suffering for the Lord. Even if everyone abandons us, Jesus will give us strength and stand with us.

Someday, when Jesus comes back to set up his Kingdom, he will judge everyone—the living and the dead. But until the Lord delivers us into his heavenly Kingdom, we must carry out the ministry we are given by God and eagerly look forward to his return. All glory to God forever and ever!

✧ ✦ ✧

The Book of
TITUS

TITUS 1

Passage: "For there are many rebellious people who engage in useless talk and deceive others."

Reflection:

There are many religions that insist that people must work for their salvation. According to the Bible, this is not true. And because of this false teaching, many people are turned away from the truth.

By giving his life for us, Jesus did everything that God required to pay the penalty for our sins. When we receive him by faith as our Savior, we receive salvation and eternal life as promised by God. So stop listening to people whose minds and consciences are corrupt because they have turned away from Jesus and the truth of God's Word. Because in God's eyes, they are detestable, disobedient, and worthless for doing anything good. Rather, live a blameless life, have a strong belief in the Bible, and encourage those whose hearts are pure with the wholesome teaching it contains.

TITUS 2

Passage: "We should live in this evil world with wisdom, righteousness, and devotion to God, while we look forward with hope to that wonderful day when the glory of our great God and Savior, Jesus Christ, will be revealed."

Reflection:

Jesus Christ gave his life to free us from sin, to cleanse us, and to make us his very own people. Therefore, we should turn from godless living and sinful pleasures and be committed to doing good. As people who belong to Jesus, we should live in a way that honors God and is an example for others. So let's live a good life characterized by trustworthiness and integrity and make Jesus, our Savior, attractive to the world in every way.

TITUS 3

Passage: "Once we, too, were foolish and disobedient."

Reflection:

We, the children of God, were once slaves to sinful lusts and pleasures. Our lives were full of evil, envy, and hate. But God revealed his love and kindness to us and saved us!

God did not save us because of the righteous things we did (even if there were some); he saved us because of his mercy. Jesus washed away our sins and gave us spiritual birth and spiritual life through the Holy Spirit. Because of his grace, God made us right in his sight and gave us confidence that we will inherit eternal life.

May we who trust in God be productive and devote ourselves to doing good. May we always be ready to meet the urgent needs of others. And may we be gentle and show true humility to everyone.

✧ ✧ ✧

The Book of
PHILEMON

PHILEMON

Passage: "Your love has given me much joy and comfort, my brother, for your kindness has often refreshed the hearts of God's people."

Reflection:

As beloved children of God whose souls have been saved by putting our faith in the Lord Jesus, the least we can do is to love God's people. As we understand that Jesus paid for all of our sin with his blood and we owe nothing, we can put into action the generosity that comes from our faith. And as we experience all the good things we have in Christ, we can show kindness to our brothers and sisters in the Lord. Then their hearts will be refreshed and comforted by the love of Jesus they receive through us.

May God the Father and the Lord Jesus Christ give you grace and peace.

✦ ✦ ✦

The Book of
HEBREWS

Reading:

HEBREWS 1

Passage: "Long ago, God spoke many times and in
many ways to our ancestors through the
prophets. And now, in these final days, he
has spoken to us through his Son."

Reflection:

Jesus is far greater than the angels. Angels are spirit
servants sent to care for people who have accepted Jesus
and will inherit salvation. But Jesus is the Son of God.

Through Jesus, God created the universe.

Jesus radiates God's own glory and expresses the very
character of God.

Jesus sustains everything by the power of his
command.

After Jesus cleansed us from our sins, he sat down at
the place of honor in heaven—God's right hand.

God promised everything to Jesus as an inheritance.

The name of Jesus is greater than any other name.

Jesus will live forever, and his throne will endure
forever and ever. Amen!

HEBREWS 2

Passage: "Because God's children are human beings—made of flesh and blood—the Son also became flesh and blood. For only as a human being could he die, and only by dying could he break the power of the devil, who had the power of death. Only in this way could he set free all who have lived their lives as slaves to the fear of dying."

Reflection:

Do you have a fear of dying? The Bible says that we cannot escape death if we ignore the gift of salvation that was first announced by the Lord Jesus himself. Jesus came down from heaven to help us, so he became like us in every way. Jesus went through suffering and testing, so he is able to help us when we are suffering and being tested. And Jesus tasted death for everyone so that many people will be brought into glory. When Jesus is your Savior-brother and God is your Father, there is freedom from the fear of dying because you are part of God's forever family, and you have been given the gift of everlasting life.

HEBREWS 3

Passage: "You must warn each other every day while it is still 'today,' so that none of you will be deceived by sin and hardened against God."

Reflection:

When you hear the voice of the Holy Spirit urging you to come to Jesus, don't harden your heart and turn away from God like Israel did when they were in the wilderness. They heard God's voice, but they didn't listen. Because they rebelled and tried his patience, God was angry with the sinful Israelites, and their corpses lay in the wilderness. Their disobedience and unbelief prevented them from entering God's rest.

Today, when God touches your heart and mind and nudges you to repent of your sin, respond in obedience. Believe in Jesus, who oversees God's entire house, and you will be forgiven. But if you choose to turn away from the living God, you will not be allowed to enter his eternal rest.

HEBREWS 4

Passage: "Nothing in all creation is hidden from God. Everything is naked and exposed before his eyes, and he is the one to whom we are accountable."

Reflection:

The Bible, the written Word of God, is alive and powerful. It exposes our innermost thoughts and desires. It is sharper than the sharpest two-edged sword. And it cuts between soul and spirit.

God's Word teaches us about faith, salvation, and how we ought to live as obedient people of God. And those who listen to God and put their faith in Jesus Christ will receive salvation. They will enter the special place of rest when their work on earth is done—like God rested after creating the world. But until that day of rest, may we hold firmly to what we believe and go to Jesus, our great High Priest, when we are weak. Jesus understands everything perfectly, and he will give us mercy and grace to help us when we boldly bring our requests to the throne of our gracious God.

HEBREWS 5

Passage: "While Jesus was here on earth, he offered prayers and pleadings, with a loud cry and tears, to the one who could rescue him from death. And God heard his prayers because of his deep reverence for God."

Reflection:

Even though Jesus is God's Son, he learned obedience from the things he suffered. So God chose Jesus, who never sinned, as the perfect High Priest and the source of eternal salvation. So everyone who accepts Jesus as their Savior will be rescued from death, and their prayers will be heard by God.

As believers in Jesus Christ, may our daily diet be the truth of the Bible. May we progress from the milk to the solid food of Scripture. And may we grow from infants who don't know how to do what is right to mature Christians who have the skill to know the difference between right and wrong.

HEBREWS 6

Passage: "...it is impossible for God to lie."

Reflection:

Since it is impossible for God to lie and he has given us his promises, we who have fled to Jesus for salvation can have great confidence and hope in the future. This hope is a strong and trustworthy anchor for our souls. And as we wait patiently, like Abraham did, we can be sure that we will inherit what God promised because of our faith and endurance.

God is not unjust. He will not forget how hard we work for him and show our love to him by caring for others. For we who have repented from our sin and evil deeds and have placed our faith in Christ are meant for better things—things that come with salvation—and God will certainly bless us, both in this life and in the life to come.

HEBREWS 7

Passage: "But because Jesus lives forever, his priesthood lasts forever. Therefore, he is able, once and forever, to save those who come to God through him. He lives forever to intercede with God on their behalf."

Reflection:

Jesus is holy and blameless and unstained by sin. He has been set apart from sinners and has been given the highest place of honor in heaven by God.

Death prevents priests from remaining in office, but Jesus lives forever. All people, including priests, must regularly repent for their sins. But Jesus never had to repent because he never sinned.

Jesus gave his own body as a sacrifice for people's sins—one perfect sacrifice that will last forever. So once we come to God through Jesus, we are saved forever, and he will forever intercede with God on our behalf. Jesus is the only High Priest we will ever need.

HEBREWS 8

Passage: "But now Jesus, our High Priest, has been given a ministry that is far superior to the old priesthood, for he is the one who mediates for us a far better covenant with God, based on better promises."

Reflection:

Jesus Christ, our High Priest, ministers to God the Father in the heavenly Tabernacle that was built by the Lord, not by human hands. Priests on earth serve in a system that is only a copy or a shadow of the real one in heaven.

When a person belongs to Christ, their old life is replaced with a new life. When God made a new covenant through Jesus, his Son, he made the first covenant obsolete. So those who follow the law of Moses are following a system that is out of date and will soon disappear. For if the first covenant was perfectly faultless, God would not have replaced it—but he did—through Jesus Christ.

HEBREWS 9

Passage: "And just as each person is destined to die once and after that comes judgment, so also Christ was offered once for all time as a sacrifice to take away the sins of many people."

Reflection:

Without the shedding of blood, there is no forgiveness of sins. Under the old system, the blood of goats and bulls could cleanse people's bodies from ceremonial impurity. But under the new system, the blood of Jesus Christ purifies our consciences from sinful deeds.

Christ died once to set us free from the penalty of sin so that we can receive the eternal inheritance God promised to us. Then he entered into heaven where he now appears before God the Father on our behalf. And Jesus will soon come again, not to deal with our sins, but to bring salvation to all who are called and are eagerly waiting for him!

HEBREWS 10

Passage: "It's a terrible thing to fall into the hands of the living God."

Reflection:

Before Christ came, anyone who refused to obey the law of Moses was put to death without mercy based on the testimony of two or three witnesses. But now, the punishment will be much worse for people who have trampled on the Son of God and have treated his blood, which makes us holy, as if it were common and unholy. God will pay them back with judgment and raging fire for rejecting his Son.

God can be trusted to keep his promises. Therefore, we who confidently believe in the Lord Jesus must continue to do God's will, hold tightly to our hope, and live by faith despite suffering. Because in just a little while, our patient endurance will result in a great reward. For we are not like those who turn away from God to their own destruction. We are the faithful children of God whose souls will be saved.

HEBREWS 11

Passage: "Faith is the confidence that what we hope for will actually happen; it gives us assurance about things we cannot see."

Reflection:

It is impossible to please God without faith. For anyone who wants to come to God must believe that he exists and that he rewards those who sincerely seek him.

By faith, we understand that the universe was formed at God's command.

By faith, we obey God, even though sometimes it doesn't make sense, and we don't always know where we are going.

By faith, we believe that God will keep his promises.

By faith, we do not fear, and our weakness is turned to strength because we keep our eyes on the One who is invisible.

By faith, we live as foreigners here on earth, looking forward to everlasting life in a heavenly homeland—a city with eternal foundations that is designed and built by God.

HEBREWS 12

Passage: "For the Lord disciplines those he loves..."

Reflection:

Who ever heard of a child who is never disciplined by its father? In the same way, those whom God accepts as his children will receive—and should submit to—his divine discipline. Our heavenly Father's discipline is painful, but it is always good for us, and it will result in peaceful, right living.

When life is a struggle, don't become weary and give up. And don't refuse to listen to the One who is always speaking. Strip off the sin that trips you up, keep your eyes on Jesus, and run with endurance the race that God has set. Think of all the hostility that Jesus endured. Is your life so hard that you have died like Jesus did?

So please God by obeying him and worshiping him with holy fear and awe. Work at living in peace with everyone. And be thankful that your name is written in heaven.

HEBREWS 13

Passage: "These are the sacrifices that please God."

Reflection:
- Do not be attracted by strange, new ideas.
- Keep on loving each other as brothers and sisters.
- Show hospitality.
- Remember those in prison.
- Remember people who are being mistreated.
- Remember your leaders who taught you the Word of God.
- Remain faithful in marriage.
- Don't love money. Be satisfied with what you have.
- Do good and share with those in need.
- Obey your spiritual leaders.
- Pray that you will have a clear conscience and live honorably.

Remember, Jesus Christ is the same yesterday, today, and forever. He will never fail you or abandon you.

May the God of peace produce in you every good thing that is pleasing to him. And may God's grace be with you always.

❖ ❖ ❖

The Book of
JAMES

JAMES 1

Passage: "Dear brothers and sisters, when troubles of any kind come your way, consider it an opportunity for great joy."

Reflection:

Troubles test our faith in God and help us grow in our endurance. Temptation comes from our own desires (not from God), which entice us, drag us away, and lead to sinful actions. When we patiently endure testing, troubles, and temptation, God will bless us with the crown of life. So be sure your faith is in God alone—not divided between God and the world.

Anger does not produce the righteousness that God desires. So we must be quick to listen, slow to speak, and slow to get angry. And as followers of Jesus, we must get rid of all filth and evil in our lives and refuse to let the world corrupt us.

Whatever is good and perfect is a gift to us from God our Father. He never changes, and neither does his Word, which has the power to save your soul. So don't just listen to the Bible, do what it says, and God will bless you.

JAMES 2

Passage: "What good is it, dear brothers and sisters, if you say you have faith but don't show it by your actions? Can that kind of faith save anyone?"

Reflection:

Faith by itself is dead and useless unless it produces good deeds. For example, if a brother or sister is in need of food or clothing but you don't give them what they need, what good does that do?

Abraham is another example of faith and deeds working together. He believed God and put his faith in action by doing what God told him to do. Rahab was also shown to be right with God by her actions.

Today and every day, may our beliefs and behaviors be in alignment. For just as the body is dead without breath, so also faith is dead without good works.

JAMES 3

Passage: "For wherever there is jealousy and selfish ambition, there you will find disorder and evil of every kind."

Reflection:

Jealousy and selfishness are not God's kind of wisdom; they are earthly, unspiritual, and demonic. Wisdom from God is pure, peace-loving, gentle, humble, and willing to yield to others. It is sincere, full of mercy and good deeds, and shows no favoritism.

Living with godly wisdom includes controlling our tongues. For the tongue is like a flame that can set your whole life on fire. One minute, it praises God, and the next minute, it curses people who are made in the image of God. If we can control our tongues, texting, and typing, we can also control ourselves in every other way.

Therefore, as children of God, let's prove we are wise with wisdom from above by living honorable lives and planting seeds of peace.

JAMES 4

Passage: "Remember, it is sin to know what you ought to do and then not do it."

Reflection:

God is passionate that the Holy Spirit he placed within us who have accepted Jesus as our Savior should be faithful to him. So wash your hands and hearts of sin, come close to God, and resist the devil. Don't let your loyalty be divided between God and the world because friendship with the world makes you an enemy of God.

Don't criticize, judge, or speak evil against others. Our job is to obey God and leave the judging to him. God alone is the Judge, and he alone has the power to save or destroy. We have no right to judge others.

Don't make plans and boast about what you will do in the future. How do you know what your life will be like tomorrow? You don't. God's will determines your future, not your pretentious plans. So put your confidence in God and trust his plan for your life—his good and perfect plan.

JAMES 5

Passage: "Are any of you suffering hardships? You should pray."

Reflection:

Prayer is a key activity in the life of a believer. When we or others are suffering, we should take it to our Father in prayer. Because prayers offered in faith by a righteous person have great power and produce wonderful results.

We must also have patience as we wait for God to answer our prayers. Job was a man who had patience in suffering. He had great endurance, and now he receives great honor. And as farmers pray for rain and look forward to a bountiful harvest, Christians must pray for the souls of the lost and wait patiently for their salvation. So, let's be persistent in prayer, patient in suffering, and take courage in hardships for the coming of the Lord is near!

✧ ✧ ✧

The Book of
1 PETER

1 PETER 1

Passage: "For you have been born again, but not to a
life that will quickly end. Your new life will
last forever because it comes from the eternal,
living word of God."

Reflection:

We, as believers, were chosen by God and have been
cleansed from our sins by the precious blood of Jesus
Christ, the sinless, spotless Lamb of God. By God's
mercy, we have been born again and can look forward
to a priceless inheritance and eternal life. But while we
anticipate the wonderful joy ahead, we must also endure
many trials. Like fire tests and purifies gold, these trials
will test, purify, and strengthen our faith, proving that
it is genuine.

During our time as temporary residents of earth, we
must live as God's obedient children and be careful not
to slip back into our old way of living. May God give
us more and more grace and peace as we live in reverent
fear of him, exercise self-control, and put all our faith,
hope, and trust in Jesus.

1 PETER 2

Passage: "But you are not like that, for you are a chosen people. You are royal priests, a holy nation, God's very own possession. As a result, you can show others the goodness of God, for he called you out of the darkness into his wonderful light."

Reflection:

Once we had no identity as a people, but now, we who trust Jesus are God's people. As we live on earth as temporary residents and foreigners, our Father warns us to keep away from worldly desires and live properly among unbelievers. We must also submit to all human authority, respect everyone, fear God, and love the family of believers.

God is pleased when we patiently endure unjust treatment because we are called to do good—even if it means suffering—just as Christ, our example, suffered for us. Jesus did not retaliate or threaten revenge when he was treated unfairly. Our Lord left his case in the hands of God, just as we who live in the light should also do.

1 PETER 3

Passage: "The eyes of the Lord watch over those who
do right, and his ears are open to their prayers.
But the Lord turns his face against those who
do evil."

Reflection:

As people who belong to Christ, we should do what
is right and good, without fear of what others might do
or say, such as:

- Live pure and reverent lives.
- Honor each other.
- Treat others with understanding.
- Be of one mind.
- Sympathize with each other.
- Love each other as brothers and sisters.
- Have a gentle spirit and a tender heart.
- Keep a humble attitude.
- Don't repay evil with evil.
- Don't retaliate with insults when you are insulted.
- Keep from speaking evil and telling lies.
- Search for peace and work to keep it.
- Worship Christ as Lord of your life.

1 PETER 4

Passage: "So if you are suffering in a manner that pleases God, keep on doing what is right, and trust your lives to the God who created you, for he will never fail you."

Reflection:

When you have suffered physically for Christ, you have finished with sin, and you will be anxious to do the will of God. Jesus Christ suffered physical pain, so you must be ready to suffer, too.

There is no shame in suffering for being a Christian. The fiery trials that you endure as a follower of Christ make you a partner with Jesus in his suffering. So, if you are insulted because you are a believer, you will be blessed. And because of your suffering, you will experience the wonderful joy of seeing the glory of Jesus Christ when it is revealed to all the world. Praise God for the privilege of being called by his name!

Remember, the end of the world—and the gracious salvation of God's household—is coming soon. All glory and power to God forever and ever! Amen.

1 PETER 5

Passage: "In his kindness, God called you to share in his eternal glory by means of Christ Jesus. So after you have suffered a little while, he will restore, support, and strengthen you, and he will place you on a firm foundation."

Reflection:

To our family of believers all over the world—

May you be strong in your faith and stand firm against the devil, who prowls around like a lion.

May you care for the people that God has entrusted to you, leading them by your own good example.

May you give all your worries and cares to God.

May you dress yourself in humility instead of pride as you relate to one another.

May you humble yourself under the mighty power of God, who will lift you up in honor at just the right time.

May you stand firm in God's grace.

And may the peace of Christ be with you all.

✧ ✧ ✧

The Book of
2 PETER

2 PETER 1

Passage: "By his divine power, God has given us everything we need for living a godly life. We have received all of this by coming to know him, the one who called us to himself by means of his marvelous glory and excellence."

Reflection:

Once we were in a dark place, but the day has dawned, and Christ, the Morning Star now shines in our hearts. We are the people whom God has called, chosen, and cleansed from our sins. And we have received great and precious promises from God. These promises enable us to share God's divine nature and escape the world's corruption. So, we must respond to God's promises and develop into mature followers of Jesus Christ.

The more we grow, the more productive and useful we will be to the Kingdom of God. Our growth should follow this pattern: faith à moral excellence à knowledge à self-control à patient endurance à godliness à affection for brothers and sisters in Christ à love for everyone.

May God give you more and more grace and peace as you grow in your knowledge of him. And when it's time for you to leave this earthly life, may God give you a grand entrance into the eternal Kingdom of our Lord and Savior Jesus Christ.

2 PETER 2

Passage: "So you see, the Lord knows how to rescue godly people from their trials, even while keeping the wicked under punishment until the day of final judgment."

Reflection:

God protected Noah (who warned the world of God's righteous judgment) and the seven others in his family when he destroyed the world of ungodly people with a flood. God also recued Lot, a righteous man, out of Sodom before he turned the cities of Sodom and Gomorrah into heaps of ashes because of the shameful immorality of the wicked people there. These are two examples of what happens to ungodly people, especially those with twisted sexual desires and those who despise authority.

People are slaves to whatever controls them. And those who are slaves of sin and corruption live under God's curse and are doomed to blackest darkness.

2 PETER 3

Passage: "But you must not forget this one thing, dear friends: A day is like a thousand years to the Lord, and a thousand years is like a day. The Lord isn't really being slow about his promise, as some people think. No, he is being patient for your sake. He does not want anyone to be destroyed but wants everyone to repent."

Reflection:

The day of the Lord will come as unexpectedly as a thief. It is the day when God will set the heavens on fire, and the earth and its elements will melt away in the flames. It is the day of judgment when ungodly people will be destroyed.

Since everything around us is going to be destroyed, we should live peaceful, pure, and holy lives. Don't make the things of this world your god. For believers can look forward to the day of the Lord and the promise of the new heavens and a new earth that is filled with the righteousness of God.

And remember, the Lord's patience gives people time to be saved—but one day, his patience will run out.

✧ ✧ ✧

The Book of
1 JOHN

1 JOHN 1

Passage: "If we confess our sins, He is faithful and righteous to forgive us our sins and to cleanse us from all unrighteousness."

Reflection:

If we claim we have no sin, we are only fooling ourselves, and we are calling God a liar.

God is light, and there is no darkness in him at all. Sin is darkness. So, we cannot have fellowship with God unless we are living in the light with him. Only the blood of Jesus can cleanse us from sin and spiritual darkness and bring us into the light. Anyone who claims to have fellowship with God but goes on living in sin is lying.

Christians can never lose their relationship to God. Once we receive the gift of salvation by asking Jesus into our hearts, we are always God's children. But like a child who disobeys their parents creates friction and distance, if we disobey God by sinning (in our thoughts, words, or actions), it gets in the way of our fellowship. So, we must regularly confess our sin and be forgiven in order to restore close fellowship with our heavenly Father.

1 JOHN 2

Passage: "But those who obey God's word truly show how completely they love him. That is how we know we are living in him. Those who say they live in God should live their lives as Jesus did."

Reflection:

Jesus lived the truth of the commandment to love one another. And he, the One who is truly righteous, is the sacrifice that pays the penalty for our sins and the sins of the whole world.

Anyone who says that Jesus is not the Messiah, and anyone who denies the Father and the Son is an antichrist. Anyone who denies Jesus, the Son, doesn't have the Father. But anyone who acknowledges and accepts the Son also has the Father.

Christians who have believed and received Jesus Christ as their Savior have been given his Holy Spirit. The Spirit lives within us and teaches us what we need to know and what is true. And since we are living in the last hour, we should remain in fellowship with Christ through his Spirit and not love the world or the things it offers. For the world and everything that people crave are fading away. But God's children—whose sins have been forgiven through Jesus and who do what pleases God—will live forever.

1 JOHN 3

Passage: "See how very much our Father loves us, for he calls us his children, and that is what we are!"

Reflection:

Those who have been born into God's family do not make a practice of sinning because God's life is in them. In fact, they can't keep on sinning because they are children of God. When people keep on sinning, it shows that they belong to the devil, who has been sinning from the beginning of time. But Jesus came to destroy the works of the devil.

This is how we can tell who are children of God and who are children of the devil:

Anyone who does not live righteously and does not love other believers does not belong to God. So don't be surprised, Christian brothers and sisters, if the world hates you. For those who belong to the evil one and do what is evil often hate those who belong to Jesus and do what is righteous.

1 JOHN 4

Passage: "God showed how much he loved us by sending his one and only Son into the world so that we might have eternal life through him. This is real love—not that we loved God, but that he loved us and sent his Son as a sacrifice to take away our sins."

Reflection:

God is love.

Anyone who does not love does not know God. Anyone who does not declare that Jesus is the Son of God does not have God living in them. They have the spirit of deception, and they are not from God. They speak from the world's viewpoint, and the world listens to them.

But we belong to God. And God has given believers his Spirit as proof that we live in him, and he lives in us. And the Spirit who lives in us—the Spirit of truth—is greater than the spirit who lives in the world.

As we live in God, may our love grow more perfect. As we trust in his perfect love, may all fear be expelled. And as we live like Jesus here in this world, may we love each other more and more.

1 JOHN 5

Passage: "And this is what God has testified: He has given us eternal life, and this life is in his Son. Whoever has the Son has life; whoever does not have God's Son does not have life."

Reflection:

Every child of God defeats this evil world through our faith. Yes, only those who believe that Jesus is the Son of God can win the battle against the world. And everyone who believes in the name of Jesus can know without a doubt that they have eternal life.

As God's children, we can be confident that our heavenly Father hears our prayers. We also know that God forever holds us securely and that the evil one, who controls the world around us, cannot touch us. So keep away from anything that might take God's place in your heart, obey him, and live in fellowship with the only true God and with his Son, Jesus Christ.

✧ ✧ ✧

The Book of
2 JOHN

2 JOHN

Passage: "Love means doing what God has commanded us, and he has commanded us to love one another, just as you heard from the beginning."

Reflection:

The Holy Spirit of truth lives in followers of Jesus Christ, and he will be with us forever. However, in this world, there are many deceivers and antichrists. So be diligent to love God and love others but be careful not to follow or encourage the evil teachings of those who deny Jesus Christ. For anyone who denies Jesus does not have a relationship with God.

May grace, mercy, and peace continue to be with the chosen people of God who live in truth and love.

✦ ✧ ✦

The Book of
3 JOHN

3 JOHN

Passage: "Dear friend, I hope all is well with you and that you are as healthy in body as you are strong in spirit."

Reflection:

May you, a beloved child of God, live according to the truth.

May you be faithful to God and care for other believers—even those who are strangers to you.

May you have loving friendships with other Christians.

And may you support and provide for your spiritual teachers in a way that pleases God.

May you follow only what is good and not be influenced by bad examples of evil people who do not know God.

May you always speak the truth and look forward to seeing Jesus face to face.

Peace be with you, dear friend.

✧ ✧ ✧

The Book of
JUDE

JUDE

Passage: "... some ungodly people have wormed their way into your churches, saying that God's marvelous grace allows us to live immoral lives. The condemnation of such people was recorded long ago, for they have denied our only Master and Lord, Jesus Christ."

Reflection:

What sorrow awaits people who practice immorality and sexual perversion and who have brought it into God's church, creating division. They are like unthinking animals who do whatever their instincts tell them because they do not have God's Spirit in them. They are shameless shepherds, doubly dead trees that bear no fruit, and dangerous reefs that can shipwreck you. They are doomed forever to the blackest darkness.

What should Christians who have been called by God do?

Defend the faith. Build each other up. Pray in the power of the Holy Spirit. Hate the sins that contaminate the lives of people but show the sinner mercy by cautiously trying to rescue them from the flames of judgment. And remember, God the Father loves you and keeps you safe in the care of Jesus Christ.

"Now all glory to God, who is able to keep you from falling away and will bring you with great joy into his glorious presence without a single fault. All glory to him who alone is God, our Savior through Jesus Christ our Lord. All glory, majesty, power, and authority are his before all time, and in the present, and beyond all time! Amen."

✧ ✧ ✧

The Book of
REVELATION

REVELATION 1

Passage: "God blesses the one who reads the words of this prophecy to the church, and he blesses all who listen to its message and obey what it says, for the time is near."

Reflection:

While John was exiled on the island of Patmos for testifying about Jesus and preaching God's Word, Jesus appeared to him and instructed him to write down everything that was revealed to him about the future events that will soon take place.

John described Jesus as wearing a long robe with a gold sash across his chest. His hair was as white as snow, and his eyes were like flames of fire. His feet were like polished bronze, and his voice thundered. His face was like the sun in all its brilliance.

Jesus is the ruler of all the kings of the world. He is the Alpha and Omega—the beginning and the end. He is the Almighty One who always was, who is, and who is still to come. And Jesus holds the keys to death and the grave.

Jesus Christ, the one who loves us and freed us from our sins by shedding his blood, is the faithful witness to all the things to come. He died, was the first to rise from the dead, and he is alive forever and ever! And soon, everyone will see Jesus return with the clouds of heaven! Yes! Amen!

REVELATION 2

Passage: "Anyone with ears to hear must listen to the Spirit and understand what he is saying to the churches."

Reflection:

Jesus knows all the things we do. He knows all about our suffering and the blasphemy of those who oppose Christians. He knows that we live in a world where Satan has his throne.

Jesus sees our hard work. He sees when we suffer for him. He sees our loyalty and refusal to deny him. He sees the constant improvement we make in our love, our faith, our service, and our patient endurance.

What does Jesus promise to everyone who is victorious in him?

- We will not be harmed by the second death—the lake of fire.
- We will get to eat delicious fruit from the tree of life in the paradise of God.
- We will also enjoy eating special manna that has been hidden away in heaven.
- We will be presented with a beautiful white stone that has our new name engraved on it.

- We will be awarded the crown of life for remaining faithful to Jesus, even when facing death.
- We will be given authority to rule over the nations with Jesus.
- And to top it off, Jesus will also give us the morning star!

The Bible is 100% accurate, and so are its prophecies. And that should cause us to sit up and pay close attention to what Jesus is saying.

REVELATION 3

Passage: "All who are victorious will be clothed in
white. I will never erase their names from the
Book of Life, but I will announce before my
Father and his angels that they are mine."

Reflection:

Jesus promises that people who belong to him prior
to the tribulation times will be protected by him from
that great time of testing that is coming upon the whole
world. We will become pillars in the Temple of God and
will never have to leave it. We will be citizens in the new
Jerusalem, the city of God that will come down from
heaven. We will walk with Jesus, wearing white and his
new name. And we will sit with Jesus on his throne—
because we are worthy.

Jesus is coming soon! And this is exciting news for
those who belong to him—the true children of God. But
for people who have not opened the door and invited
Jesus into their heart, he says, "Look! I stand at the
door and knock. If you hear my voice and open the
door, I will come in, and we will share a meal together
as friends."

Open the door.

REVELATION 4

Passage: "I saw a throne in heaven and someone sitting on it."

Reflection:

Jesus Christ is sitting on the throne in heaven, ruling and reigning over all things. He looks brilliant as gemstones, and the glow of an emerald circles his throne like a rainbow.

From the throne of Christ comes flashes of lightning and rumbles of thunder. In front of the throne is a shiny sea of glass that sparkles like crystal. There are also seven torches with burning flames, representing the sevenfold Spirit of God.

Surrounding the throne are twenty-four thrones with elders clothed in white sitting on them. Each elder is wearing a gold crown.

In the center and around the throne are four living beings that look like a lion, an ox, something with a human face, and an eagle in flight. Each being has six wings, which are covered with eyes, inside and out. Day after day and night after night, the living beings give glory, honor, and thanks to Jesus.

The throne in heaven is not empty. It is occupied by Jesus Christ, our Lord and Creator. May our worship of the King reflect his worthiness, holiness, honor, glory, and power.

Reading:

REVELATION 5

Passage: "Stop weeping! Look, the Lion of the tribe of
Judah, the heir to David's throne, has won the
victory. He is worthy to open the scroll and
its seven seals."

Reflection:

Jesus Christ, the Lamb of God who was slaughtered,
is the only one who is worthy to take the scroll containing
the world's judgments and break open its seven seals. For
his blood has ransomed people for God from every tribe,
language, people, and nation.

May we sing this mighty chorus along with millions
of angels and every creature on earth, under the earth,
and in the sea:

"Worthy is the Lamb who was slaughtered— to
receive power and riches and wisdom and strength and
honor and glory and blessing."

"Blessing and honor and glory and power belong to
the one sitting on the throne and to the Lamb forever
and ever!"

REVELATION 6

Passage: "As I watched, the Lamb broke the first of the seven seals on the scroll. Then I heard one of the four living beings say with a voice like thunder, 'Come!'"

Reflection:

When the day of God's wrath finally arrives, the four living beings will call for the four horsemen of the apocalypse to "Come!" after Jesus Christ breaks each of the first four seals.

Seal 1

A white horse with a rider who carries a bow and wears a crown on his head. This seal introduces the antichrist. He will deceive many with talks of peace, but he will wage war with people who become Christians during the tribulation.

Seal 2

A red horse with a rider who is given a sword and the authority to take peace from the earth. There will be war and slaughter everywhere.

Seal 3

A black horse with a rider who is holding a pair of scales. Famine will be so severe that a loaf of bread will cost a day's pay.

Seal 4

A green horse whose rider is named Death and his companion is the Grave will be given authority to kill one-fourth of the earth with the sword, famine, disease, and wild animals.

Seal 5

When this seal is broken, the Lord Jesus will give a white robe to the martyrs in heaven. They will be told to wait a little longer until the remaining martyrs join them. Then, at last, the Lord will avenge their blood.

Seal 6

There will be a great earthquake. The sun will turn black. The moon will turn red. The stars will fall to the earth. And the sky will roll up. All the people, from great to small, will run and try to hide from the wrath of God!

REVELATION 7

Passage: And I saw another angel coming up from the east, carrying the seal of the living God. And he shouted to those four angels, who had been given power to harm land and sea, "Wait! Don't harm the land or the sea or the trees until we have placed the seal of God on the foreheads of his servants."

Reflection:

God will place his seal on the foreheads of 144,000 people (12,000 from each of the twelve tribes of Israel) before anything on land or sea is harmed. These Jewish evangelists will spread the Good News of salvation through Jesus Christ during the tribulation.

Many people who become Christians during the tribulation will lose their lives, but they will be given eternal life. They will never again experience hunger, thirst, or the scorching heat of the sun in its final days. And God will wipe every tear from their eyes. They will be forever clothed in white robes, worshiping and serving God in his heavenly Temple. And Jesus, the Lamb on the throne, will be the Shepherd who leads these tribulation saints to springs of life-giving water!

REVELATION 8

Passage: "When the Lamb broke the seventh seal on the scroll, there was silence throughout heaven for about half an hour. I saw the seven angels who stand before God, and they were given seven trumpets."

Reflection:

Seal 7

The seventh seal will usher in the seven trumpet judgments, which will begin after the earth suffers a terrible earthquake.

Trumpet 1

Hail and fire mixed with blood will be thrown down on the earth. One-third of the earth will be set on fire. All the green grass and one-third of the trees will be burned.

Trumpet 2

A great mountain of fire will be thrown into the sea, causing one-third of the ships and sea creatures to be destroyed. One-third of the water in the sea will become blood.

Trumpet 3

A great star called Bitterness will fall into one-third of the fresh water. Many people will die from drinking the bitter water.

Trumpet 4

One-third of the sun, moon, and stars will become dark. There will be one-third less light in the day and night.

"Terror, terror, terror to all who belong to this world..."

REVELATION 9

Passage: "But the people who did not die in these plagues still refused to repent of their evil deeds and turn to God."

Reflection:

Trumpet 5

The demonic angel named Abaddon—the Destroyer—will be given the key to open the bottomless pit. Then, the earth's sun and air will turn dark as the smoke billows out of the pit. Locusts that look like horses with human faces, women's hair, and lion's teeth will emerge from the smoke. With their tails, they will sting like scorpions the people who do not have the seal of God on their foreheads. People will long to die, but they will have to endure this torture for five months!

Trumpet 6

A demonically inspired, 200-million-man army will kill one-third of all the people on earth with fire, smoke, and burning sulfur.

The hearts of unbelievers, who are held captive by Satan, will be so hardened against God in the great tribulation that the people who are alive after enduring these torturous plagues will still not be persuaded to turn to Christ and repent of their sins.

REVELATION 10

Passage: "There will be no more delay. When the seventh angel blows his trumpet, God's mysterious plan will be fulfilled. It will happen just as he announced it to his servants the prophets."

Reflection:

Just as John saw, one day, there will be a mighty angel who will come down from heaven to earth. His head will be surrounded by a rainbow, which is a sign of God's mercy and faithfulness to his covenant promise.

The angel that descends from the presence of God will stand with one foot on land and one foot on the sea. This demonstrates God's ownership of the earth, which has been under Satan's control.

The angel will raise his hand toward heaven, invoking the sovereignty of God over his creation and announce that there will be no more delay. This is sweet news to the children of God, but bitter news to those who reject Jesus because God's prophetic clock will run out and there will be no more time for the people living on the earth to repent.

REVELATION 11

Passage: "It is time to judge the dead and reward your servants the prophets, as well as your holy people, and all who fear your name, from the least to the greatest."

Reflection:

During the great tribulation, God will send two prophets from heaven to witness in Jerusalem for 1,260 days. They will be clothed in burlap, and anyone who tries to harm them will be consumed by fire from their mouths. God will give them power to stop the rain, turn rivers and oceans into blood, and strike the earth with plagues. Eventually, the beast will kill them—but not until they complete their testimony. People will stare and gloat over their dead bodies for three and a half days. Then God will breathe life into them. They will stand up and be raised up to heaven in a cloud as their enemies watch! At the same time, seven thousand people will die in Jerusalem during an earthquake that will destroy a tenth of the city.

Trumpet 7

Then, an angel will blow his trumpet and announce that the world has now become the Kingdom of our God. The victory is still future, but to God who sees all things—past, present, and future—the victory has already happened!

And as the doors of the Temple of God open in heaven, lightning will flash, thunder will crash and roar, there will be a terrible hailstorm, and the earth will shake violently.

REVELATION 12

Passage: "But terror will come on the earth and the sea, for the devil has come down to you in great anger, knowing that he has little time."

Reflection:

Satan is referred to as a large red dragon in the book of Revelation. He is not more powerful than God, but he is fierce, aggressive, and out for blood. Satan, formerly the angel named Lucifer, was thrown down from heaven to earth by God—along with all his evil angels—and he is the one who is deceiving the whole world. As pictured in the war in heaven that John saw, Satan did everything he could to prevent Jesus Christ from being born into the messianic line of Israel (pictured as the woman). But Jesus was born, and he defeated sin, death, and Satan at the cross!

Today, Satan has access to God. His nickname is the Accuser because he accuses Christians of sin before God—day and night. Thankfully, Jesus also has access to God, and he defends as innocent everyone whose sins have been covered by his blood.

Because Satan is very angry at God, he has declared war on the people who belong to Jesus Christ. And as the end of the devil's time draws closer and closer, his battle against God and the children of God will continue to heat up. But remember, Satan has no more power over your life than you choose to give him. So, resist the devil and trust Jesus because heaven still rules on earth!

REVELATION 13

Passage: "Then I saw a beast rising up out of the sea."

Reflection:

The Holy Trinity is God the Father, Jesus Christ, and the Holy Spirit. The unholy trinity is Satan, the beast (also known as the antichrist), and the second beast, who is called the false prophet.

During the tribulation, the antichrist will rise from among the people on earth, referred to as the sea. He will receive his power and authority directly from Satan. And just as Satan tries to deceive people by imitating God, the antichrist will try to deceive people by imitating Jesus Christ. For that reason, the antichrist will be fatally wounded and come back to life. Then the whole world, except Christians, will give allegiance to him.

For forty-two months, the antichrist beast will blaspheme God, wage war against God's holy people, and rule every nation. The people who belong to the world will worship the beast. They are the people whose names are not written in the Lamb's Book of Life.

During this time, a second beast, who is a false prophet, will appear on the scene. He will deceive the people with miracles and exercise all the authority of the antichrist. And just as the Holy Spirit points people to

Jesus Christ, the false prophet will point people to the antichrist.

The false prophet will erect a statue of the antichrist and give the statue the ability to speak. The statue will command that everyone who refuses to worship it must die. God's holy people must remain faithful and endure persecution during this terrible time, even though many Christians will be martyred.

The false prophet will also require that everyone must receive a mark on their hand or forehead in order to buy or sell anything. Most people, choosing their stomach over their soul, will accept the mark—either the name of the antichrist or his number, which is 666. In the Bible, God's number of perfection is 7, and the number of man is 6. So, just as the antichrist's number reflects, Satan will always fall short of God.

REVELATION 14

Passage: "And I saw another angel flying through the sky..."

Reflection:

An angel from heaven will fly through the sky carrying the Good News one more time to the people of the world.

Another angel will follow, announcing that the immoral city of Babylon has fallen.

Then, a third angel will warn the people that anyone who worships the beast and his statue or accepts his mark must drink the cup of God's wrath. They will be tormented without relief by fire and burning sulfur— day and night, forever and ever. But those who die in the Lord Jesus will be eternally blessed.

Next, an angel from the Temple in heaven will shout, "Swing the sickle, for the time of harvest has come; the crop on earth is ripe." Then Jesus, the Son of Man, will swing his sickle over the whole earth.

And another angel with a sharp sickle will appear.

One more angel from the altar in heaven, who has power to destroy with fire, will tell the angel with the sharp sickle to swing his sickle and gather the grapes from the vines of the earth because they are ripe for judgment.

The unsaved people, referred to as grapes, will be loaded into the great winepress of God's wrath. And as the grapes are trampled out, blood will flow from the winepress in a stream about 180 miles long and as high as a horse's bridle!

REVELATION 15

Passage: "Then I saw in heaven another marvelous event of great significance. Seven angels were holding the seven last plagues, which would bring God's wrath to completion."

Reflection:

The victorious people who remain faithful to Christ during the tribulation—those who will not worship the beast or his statue or take the number of his name—will be presented with harps from God in heaven. Together, they will sing the songs of Moses and of the Lamb.

Then, the doors of God's Temple in heaven will be thrown wide open, revealing the smoke from his glory and power. Seven angels wearing spotless white linen and gold sashes will be handed gold bowls containing the final plagues of God's wrath—plagues which will be poured out onto the earth.

REVELATION 16

Passage: "Since they shed the blood of your holy people
and your prophets, you have given them blood
to drink. It is their just reward."

Reflection:

During the great tribulation, the seven bowls
containing God's wrath will be poured out on the earth:

Bowl 1

Horrible, malignant sores will break out on everyone
who worships the antichrist beast and his statue.

Bowl 2

Everything in the sea will die, and the sea will become
like the blood of a corpse.

Bowl 3

The rivers and springs of water will be turned to
blood.

Bowl 4

The sun will scorch everyone with its fire.

Bowl 5

The earth will be plunged into darkness as black as the sin of the people. Everyone will grind their teeth in anguish as their fear is intensified by the darkness.

Bowl 6

The Euphrates River will dry up, enabling armies to march from east to west. Then, demonic spirits will gather the rulers of the world together in Armageddon to battle against the Lord.

Bowl 7

The worst earthquake since God put people on the earth will level the mountains, make islands disappear, and cause nations to fall into heaps of rubble. And hailstones weighing about seventy-five pounds will fall onto the people.

The people will curse God who controls the plagues—but will they repent of their sins and turn to God? NO!

REVELATION 17

Passage: "So the angel took me in the Spirit into the wilderness. There I saw a woman sitting on a scarlet beast that had seven heads and ten horns, and blasphemies against God were written all over it."

Reflection:

The angel showed John a prostitute sitting on a scarlet beast. This is a picture of the unholy alliance between the one-world religion and one-world government that will occur during the last days.

The false religion of the end times will cause unbelievers who have rejected the truth of God, to be spiritually seduced and led into eternal destruction. The government, led by the antichrist, will persecute and execute Christians, which is pictured as the prostitute being drunk on the blood of God's holy people. Eventually, the antichrist will turn on the false church and destroy the false religious system after he is done using it for his own purposes.

God is still in control. His plan and purposes will be carried out. His words will be fulfilled. The Lamb, who is Lord of lords and King of kings, will defeat the beast. And we—the called, chosen, and faithful ones who belong to Jesus—will be with him when it happens!

REVELATION 18

Passage: "Babylon is fallen—that great city is fallen!"

Reflection:

The kingdom of the antichrist will end abruptly. In a single day, the world economy and government will completely collapse—never to recover again. This is prophesied as the fall of Babylon.

Christians who will be alive during the great tribulation are warned not to take part in Babylon's culture, whose sin and evil deeds are piled as high as heaven. For God will do to her twice as much as she has done to others. The people, leaders, and businesses of the world will weep and mourn in great torment as they see the wealth that they valued so much disappear right before their eyes. No more music. No more stock market. No more working. No more weddings. No more light.

But the people of God, the apostles, and the prophets will rejoice over the fate of Babylon. For at last, God will have judged evil for our sakes!

REVELATION 19

Passage: "Let us be glad and rejoice and let us give honor to him. For the time has come for the wedding feast of the Lamb, and his bride has prepared herself."

Reflection:

Blessed are those who belong to Jesus. For we will attend the wedding feast of the Lamb, wearing the finest of pure white linen.

After the banquet, Jesus, with eyes like flames of fire, will prepare for war. He will put on his many crowns and his robe dipped in blood. And he will mount his majestic white horse. We will follow Jesus, also riding white horses, and witness him as he releases the fierce, righteous wrath of God. We will be there when Jesus—Faithful and True—throws the beast and the false prophet into the fiery lake of burning sulfur. We get to watch Jesus—the Word of God—as he kills the kings, generals, and armies of the world with the sharp sword from his mouth.

And the vultures will gorge themselves on the flesh of dead bodies.

Reading:

REVELATION 20

Passage: "Then death and the grave were thrown into the lake of fire. This lake of fire is the second death. And anyone whose name was not found recorded in the Book of Life was thrown into the lake of fire."

Reflection:

At the beginning of the Millennial reign of Christ on earth, Satan will be bound in chains and thrown into the bottomless pit. He will not be allowed to deceive anyone for one thousand years. However, when the one thousand years are up, Satan will be let out of his prison, and he won't waste any time deceiving the nations into joining together to fight against God. But when the devil's armies, as numerous as the sands on the seashore, surround God's beloved people, our Father will send down fire from heaven and consume them! Then Satan will be thrown into the lake of fire, joining the beast and the false prophet, and they will all be tormented day and night—forever and ever!

After Satan is destroyed, the earth and the heavens will pass away, and the final judgment will take place. This is when the dead will be raised to stand before the great white throne of Jesus Christ. The books containing people's deeds and the Book of Life will be open. All unbelievers will be judged according to what they have done, but since their names are not in the Book of Life, they will experience a second death when they are thrown into the lake of fire. This is where they will spend eternity experiencing God's punishment for rejecting Jesus Christ.

REVELATION 21

Passage: "Then I saw a new heaven and a new earth, for the old heaven and the old earth had disappeared. And the sea was also gone. And I saw the holy city, the new Jerusalem, coming down from God out of heaven like a bride beautifully dressed for her husband."

Reflection:

God himself will live with his children for eternity. There will be no sin, no evil, no death, no sorrow, no crying, and no pain in our new home.

The centerpiece of the new heaven and new earth will be the holy city, the new Jerusalem. It will shine with the glory of God and sparkle like a diamond. It will be 1,400 miles in length, width, and height. The city will be pure gold, as clear as glass, with walls built on foundations made of twelve layers of colorful precious stones. It will have twelve gates, each made of a single pearl, with the names of the twelve tribes of Israel on each gate. The gates will never be closed because there will be no night, no moon, and no sun. The city will be illuminated with the glory of Jesus Christ, the Lamb of God.

Will everyone live in the new heaven and new earth? The Bible makes it clear that only those whose names are written in the Lamb's Book of Life will inherit all these blessings and be allowed to enter. The fate of unbelievers is in the fiery lake of burning sulfur.

REVELATION 22

Passage: "Look, I am coming soon! Blessed are those who obey the words of prophecy written in this book."

Reflection:

Jesus is coming soon!
The Alpha and Omega.
The First and the Last.
The Beginning and the End.
The bright Morning Star.
The Source of David and the Heir to his throne.

Blessed are those who wash their robes with the blood of Jesus Christ, for we will be permitted to enter through the gates of the holy city. There will be a river, flowing with the crystal-clear water of life, down the center of main street from the throne of God and of the Lamb. There will be a tree of life on each side of the river, and we will eat the fruit from it. The name of Jesus will be written on our foreheads. We will see his face and worship him. The Lord God will shine on his holy people, and we will reign forever and ever!

Amen! Come, Lord Jesus!

Printed in the United States
by Baker & Taylor Publisher Services